Marketing Insights to Help Your Business GROW

from the nationally syndicated
Marketing Advisor

Peter Francese

PARAMOUNT MARKET PUBLISHING, INC.

Paramount Market Publishing, Inc.
301 S. Geneva Street, Suite 109
Ithaca, NY 14850
www.paramountbooks.com
Telephone: 607-275-8100; 888-787-8100
Facsimile: 607-275-8101

Publisher: James Madden
Editorial Director: Doris Walsh

Book design: Paperwork
All trademarks are the property of their respective companies.

Paramount Market Publishing's books are available at special discounts for bulk purchases for sales promotions or premiums. Special editions, including personalized covers, excerpts of existing books, and corporate imprints, can be created in large quantities for special needs. For more information, write to Special Markets, Paramount Market Publishing, 301 South Geneva Street, Suite 109, Ithaca, NY 14850, or e-mail editors@paramountbooks.com

Library of Congress Catalog Number:
Cataloging in Publication Data available
ISBN 0-9671439-8-5

1 2 3 4 5 6 7 8 9 0

**Marketing Insights to
Help Your Business Grow**
*is dedicated to all the great people at
Ottaway Newspapers without whose
cheerful help and support this book
would not have been possible.*

Other Marketing Books from PMP

The Kids Market: Myths & Realities

Marketing to American Latinos, Part I

The Mirrored Window: Focus Groups from a Moderator's Point of View

The Great Tween Buying Machine

Why People Buy Things They Don't Need

India Business

Marketing to American Latinos, Part II

Contents

Table of Tables

Keep a child's perspective in your mind all year

Perhaps the most wonderful thing about Christmas is watching the faces of small children as they behold the lights, the presents, and the festivities. Almost everything is fresh and new to them as they see many things for the first time. Listening to children excitedly talk about what they hope Santa will bring them is a uniquely uplifting experience.

But as we get older and further away from the holiday season, there is an unfortunate tendency to let the "been-there-done-that" attitude creep back into our tired minds. Whenever that occurs, it diminishes our ability to see things with a fresh perspective or even consider new ideas. Usually this happens so slowly that it's a bit like gradually getting the eye condition known as myopia.

Myopia in one's vision is also known as short-sightedness. Business people use the same words to describe a colleague who can't see any value in a new idea. Over 40 years ago, Theodore Levitt coined the term "marketing myopia." He cited, among others, U.S. railroad companies that squandered immense opportunity because they could not see that they were in the transportation business rather than just operating a railroad.

Short-sightedness afflicts big and small companies alike. Big companies are just the ones who make the national

America's Youngest Marketing Consultants

There are over 3 million more cute kids now than there were ten years ago. One in every seven Americans is between the ages of 1 and 10 years old, so there are lots of little marketing advisors to learn from.

	NUMBER	CHANGE 1990–2000
All children aged 1 to 10	40.2 million	+ 9.0%
Children aged 1 to 2	7.6	+ 2.0
Children aged 3 to 4	7.8	+ 5.2
Children aged 5 to 6	8.0	+ 9.9
Children aged 7 to 8	8.3	+ 16.5
Children aged 9 to 10	8.5	+ 16.0

Source: Census Bureau

news. Small firms can also suffer from marketing myopia, with equally serious results. Over time, it causes customers of any sized organization to just drift away or be enticed away by more innovative competitors.

Firms suffering from marketing myopia usually exhibit its primary symptoms: a profound satisfaction with the status quo and a deep denial of any problems. This is where a bright child is needed to point out that this particular emperor has no clothes. Many businesses could benefit from child-like questioning of their marketing strategies.

The problem with bringing children into a business setting is that their opinions are assumed to be uninformed since they have no experience or knowledge to understand the complexities of business. That, of course, is true. But it's not their naive comments that are valuable. It's the obvious questions they might ask, such as: "Why are you doing that?"

Customers can sometimes resemble children in the sense that we all too often do not really listen to them. And if we do hear them, we frequently discount their opinions as uninformed, since they obviously don't understand our business. Thinking like that means marketing myopia has set in big time.

MAKING A MENTAL SHIFT

If you suffer from visual myopia, eventually you will get a new pair of eyeglasses. The cure for marketing myopia is more complex because it requires a different mindset. And changing one's mind is a lot more difficult than changing corrective lenses.

The mental shift required to cure marketing myopia means exchanging at least three beliefs.

First: Exchange any satisfaction you may have with your present marketing for a continual desire to con-sistently improve it. An incrementally improving busi-ness will always outlast one that innovates only when it is forced to do so.

Second: Discard the thought that you know what cus-tomers want. Unless you have been listening to them carefully, chances are very small that you will guess right. There are a few marketing geniuses out there, but most of us are not. The better idea is to do some market research before investing large sums in what you think customers will buy. Gap clothing stores would be a lot better off today if they had surveyed a representative sample of their customers before radically changing their merchandise. Or better yet, if they had a program of asking former customers why they stopped coming to their stores.

Third: Periodically ask simple questions that perhaps a smart child would ask. "Is what we say (in our advertising) true?" or "Do we keep our (brand) promises?" or "How many people (customers) come back a second time?"

Continually asking questions like that shifts the focus from the internal operations of the business to the external world of present, past and future customers. Fresh ideas that can invigorate any business almost always come from outside.

Sometimes a fresh idea comes from a child who sees things that we have stopped looking at and can ask some of the silliest and at the same time most profound questions you have ever heard. So every now and then, try to look at the world from a child's perspective and then carry that thought with you all year.

I

How small businesses can use the U.S. Census

1 **Paying attention to trends pays**

Looking at demographic trends is like watching the grass grow. Nothing much happens on a day-to-day basis, but if you're not paying attention, pretty soon you're up to your waist in killer weeds. Montgomery Ward went out of business partly because, in the past, it ignored major shifts in consumer demographics.

By contrast, one reason Wal*Mart and Target are so successful is because they pay close attention to consumer and business trends and how their customers are changing. Here's some information about a couple of trends you should watch in your business.

Aging boomers

In 2002, the oldest baby boomers celebrated their 56th birthdays. Over the next 10 to 15 years, you can expect to see explosive growth of people in their 50s and early 60s. One reality is more people than ever will need to wear glasses because of deteriorating eyesight. How big is the print on all your printed material, packaging, and signs? If you expect your aging customers to read it, enlarge the print. Also, as eyes age, seeing subtle differences in shading becomes more difficult. So be sure that there is sharp contrast between printed words and images and the background—forget shading.

As people get older, they move less frequently and are more likely to spend time and money caring for their homes. But they also want to travel more and are more likely to own a vacation home. These conflicting desires suggest a growth business might be called "Property Managers, Inc." It could take care of some home maintenance for people who are away and periodically check on their homes using inexpensive web cameras.

Expect some changes in food preferences, too. Growing numbers of restaurant patrons will want choices with less fat, sugar, or salt. With increased awareness of food additives, consumers will want more details about what's in the prepared foods they're buying.

Most People Live in Metropolitan Areas

More than 8 in 10 Americans live in or near cities with 50,000 or more residents.

U.S. POPULATION, 2000 CENSUS

	POPULATION	INSIDE METROS	OUTSIDE METROS
All persons	281.4 million	80.3%	19.7%
Under age 18	72.3	80.6	19.4
Age 65 or older	35.0	76.8	23.2
Hispanic or Latino	35.3	91.1	8.9
Black or African American	34.7	86.3	13.7
Asian	10.2	95.9	4.1

Source: Census Bureau

More business start-ups

We are in a time of high demand for business and personal services as well as information services. At the same time, there are a record number of people with either past business experience or a business-school degree. The result is all-time high numbers of people either self-employed or working full- or part-time in small enterprises.

This has the effect of blurring the line between workplace and home as well as between work and leisure. It can also change consumer behavior. Time management becomes more important, and there is a heightened sense that time is money and business or work can be conducted at any time of the day or night.

Kinko's recognized this phenomenon early when it decided to open stores around the clock. Many Home Depot stores are now also open 24/7. For other businesses, it is more important than ever not to keep customers waiting on the phone or in person and to be flexible regarding business hours. Customers who take the time to come to a store become irritated when someone who phones gets priority treatment while the customer in the store waits to check out or ask a question. Make sure your employees understand your priorities.

Most businesses now on the web

The ultimate time-saving device is, of course, the internet, and virtually all start-ups have internet access. To stay competitive, your business may need a well-designed web site or at least a web page on a community site. This allows present or potential customers to learn in a few seconds, at any time, what you now offer, where you are, when you're open, and how to contact you.

Creating a web site, however, requires that you be prepared to answer customer's e-mail queries. Having a web presence without answering your e-mail is like having a huge post office box and never opening it. A customer's e-mail query doesn't have to be answered instantly, but at least within a day or two.

For all its technical wizardry, a business web site is just another way to communicate with customers and prospects. With or without it, knowing which segments of consumers are most likely to buy what you offer is what can make your business more profitable. That's because, with better knowledge of likely buyers, you can more efficiently focus your marketing efforts, regardless of how customers contact you.

Population Change—Middle Age Spread

During this decade the rate of increase for people aged 55 to 64 is projected to be about four times the average growth rate, and far above the growth rate for that age group over the past ten years.

AGE GROUP	PERCENT CHANGE 2000 TO 2010
45 to 54	+ 19%
55 to 64	+ 48
65 or older	+ 14
All ages, average	+ 10

Source: Woods & Poole Economics, Inc.

2 New census numbers add up to a marketing edge

Census numbers are like fresh fish off a boat. You don't want to let them lie around too long. While the decennial census provides valuable benchmarking data, the Census Bureau and other government agencies continually update that information with surveys, as well as projections and forecasts based on economic models. The marketing edge comes from getting this harvest of numbers and the related projections early and using them to sharpen your marketplace knowledge and get some fresh marketing ideas.

The best part about this bounty of facts is that it is virtually free. Your tax dollars paid for the collection of the data, and most of the tabulations will be put on the Census Bureau's free web site for anyone who wishes to see them. Like any big information resource, however, it helps to know what you're looking for. So here are three ideas for making the most of census data.

Describe your market area first

Before looking for any data, think about what geographic area your customers come from or could come from and define it in census geography terms. Census data are available for all residential zip codes, cities or towns, and counties. But they can also be obtained for smaller Census Bureau defined units called census tracts and block groups, which can be added together to create virtually any market area that you want to analyze.

Thinking about where your present or future customers come from will probably cause you to start asking questions about the market areas you serve. Questions such as: How many potential customers live there? Is the area growing? If so, is it above-average growth or below average? Is the market area older or younger or different in other ways from the surrounding areas that you do not serve?

For local areas, the census will still be the most complete data we have, even if many people did not fill out their census forms.

The purpose of looking at census data is to answer those questions and any others that will help you understand the consumer environment that your customers come from. The point is that if you are doing particularly well in certain places, and you have expansion plans, it makes sense to find areas that most closely match the demographics of your best market areas. That's the essence of target marketing.

Know what you want

Census data are even more useful when you begin with a clear demographic picture of your target market. Then you can focus your attention on only those census figures that describe your customers or illuminate their lifestyles. For example, if your target customers for a financial service are married couples aged 55 to 64 with an annual household income over $100,000, you will need age data, household income, and family type. Educational attainment and occupation data might also be useful.

Whatever business you are in, occasionally visiting **www.census.gov** (the Census Bureau's web site) will pay big dividends. When you go there for the first time, look in the upper left corner for the alphabet, which catalogs all census-related subjects, and click on various letters. Under the letter G is a glossary of census terms that define unfamiliar words, like *block group* and *census tract,* used in taking and tabulating the census.

The Top Three States – 1990 to 2000

One third of the nation's population growth occurred in only three states: California, Texas, and Florida. During the 1990s California grew more every six weeks than Vermont did in ten years. The Northeast region picked up only 9 percent of U.S. population growth, the Midwest had 14 percent, but the West garnered 32 percent and the South captured 45 percent.

FASTEST GROWING

Nevada	▲ 66%
Arizona	▲ 40%
Colorado	▲ 31%

BIGGEST IN 2000

California	33.9 million
Texas	20.9 million
New York	19.0 million

SLOWEST GROWING

North Dakota	▲ <1%
West Virginia	▲ <1%
Pennsylvania	▲ 3.4%

SMALLEST IN 2000

Wyoming	0.5 million
Vermont	0.6 million
Alaska	0.6 million

BIGGEST GROWTH

California	▲ 4.1 million
Texas	▲ 3.9 million
Florida	▲ 3.0 million

Source: Census Bureau, 2000 census data

You can also find a complete copy of the census question-naire in the Census 2000 section as well as information about how to obtain census maps if you need them. If you are interested in how many businesses like yours are in your county, look in the business section or in the alphabetic in-dex under *County Business Patterns.* Take some time to look around the site. It's a great resource.

Know census data's limitations

Any data-gathering operation the size of the census is far from perfect, but for local areas, this will still be the most complete data we have, even if many people did not fill out their census forms. Americans have never been more con-cerned about their privacy, and as a result, many households simply refused to return the questionnaire. Nationwide, only two out of every three households returned their cen-sus forms.

What this suggests is that you should not read too much precision into the census figures. For example, suppose the census data say there are 10,000 residents in your market area and 1,234 of them are aged 65 or older. Reporting that 12.34 percent of the market area's population is in that age group would be reading more accuracy into the census than is warranted. It should be reported as 12 percent and under-stood that if another market area had 13 percent or 11 per-cent, they would probably not be statistically different.

3

Information: a vital part of your business

In the new economy, information is not just vital. It is the critical component of virtually every product, service, and business transaction. But between product information, sales numbers, and customer data, the average business person today is flooded with information.

Managing that flood can seem like an impossible task, but the payoff from converting some of that data into valuable marketing knowledge and tools makes the task worth taking on. Because no matter what business you are in, to stay competitive and grow, you must also understand the information business.

To help you manage the information parts of your business, think about trying to water your garden with a big fire hose. Without some surge controls, you'd blast every plant right out of the ground. It's like that with information. The trick is to control the river of numbers by picking out and using only those bits of data that will help to make your business grow and let the rest flow by. Here are a few tips on how to do just that.

Ask only decisive questions

The trouble with too much information is that it creates thousands of answers for questions that may not be relevant to anything. Suppose, for example, that you have people answering the telephone. The phone system will generate daily, weekly, or monthly data pertaining to how many calls came in during each hour, where they came from, and how long each call lasted. Before analyzing that ocean of data, consider the important questions regarding any communications system.

How many customers are annoyed or turned away by having to wait on hold or by getting a busy signal? What is the nature of the calls? Do callers buy something, or are they just calling for—you guessed it—information about prices, services, products, and hours.

No matter what business you are in, to stay competitive and grow, you must also understand the information business.

Lots of information-gathering calls suggest that perhaps your web site needs to be promoted better and be more informative or perhaps your advertising materials are not conveying enough detail to convert interested prospects into buyers.

The decisive questions are the ones that, when answered, enable you to change your operations so that you get more customers and more revenue from your communications or advertising spending or other marketing-related expenses. Answers to questions not related to the success of your business may be nice to know or interesting, but a waste of your time.

Make sure your customers are well informed

One important characteristic of today's marketplace is that, for the most part, consumers want to know more about what they are buying. You can create great customer loyalty by satisfying that want and offering straightforward information about the features and benefits of what you sell, and details of customer options regarding your services or products.

Think about how many full-page advertisements or web sites you have visited that didn't tell you anything useful or make you better informed about what was being offered. Not all marketing messages are information rich, but one of the best reasons to have a robust web site is to answer your customers' questions in great detail at very low expense.

One reason customers want to be better informed is that it saves them time when researching a purchase and often enables them to buy something that more closely matches their needs. The value of such information to consumers is underscored by the fact that one of the most-visited paid web sites in the nation is that of *Consumer Reports* magazine.

Be selective about information from customers

Information about your customers is somewhat like a chemical fertilizer for your garden. The right amount will

 The U.S. Information Industry

The information industry is one of the new industrial categories developed by the Census Bureau for the 1997 Economic Census. This industry includes publishing, broadcasting, motion pictures and tele-communications, as well as information services and data processing.

Number of employees:	3.1 million
Average worker's annual pay:	$46,700
Number of firms:	120,000
Annual sales:	$623 billion

Source: Census Bureau

make your plants grow bigger, but too much can kill them. One of the big issues in gathering and using customer information today is privacy. Violating your customers' privacy can ruin your business.

A safe way to get information about customers is to tell them the direct benefit they will get from telling you something about themselves and their preferences. Also, be up front with a statement about how you intend to safeguard their information.

More important than their answers are your questions and your purpose for asking them. Every question put to a customer in this context should have a specific purpose. Prior to asking any question, think about this: based on the answers, what will you do differently? Are you willing to change your marketing messages or make operational changes such as adding services or changing prices based on customers' comments? If not, don't waste their time and yours asking the questions.

Virtually every business today is also in the information business. Understanding the value of such information and when to use it can help you get closer to your customers, serve them better, and help your business grow.

4 Invest with the trends for long-term gain

The best reason for staying on top of consumer trends is to more profitably market your goods and services. But keeping up on consumer trends can also be helpful when it's time to invest some of those profits, provided you are looking for long-term returns.

Knowledge of how consumers are changing may not be very helpful if you're a day trader. But over a five to ten year horizon, thinking about where consumers are going to spend their money next can point to growth industries and reveal investment opportunities.

Understanding what customers want or need and how they are changing is fundamental to the long-term success of any business. So the simplest way to assess whether or not a company has good growth prospects is to see how closely they pay attention to marketplace change and how they treat their customers.

Bad customer service means an uncertain future

If, like some airlines we know, a business appears to pay no attention to its customers' needs, it may be very profitable in the short term. But it will probably not be a good long-term investment as customers will soon enough find alternatives to its bad service.

On the other hand, if a company has a strong customer focus and a history of innovation in response to new customer needs, then it's likely to be a long-term winner. You can spot firms like that because their annual reports usually contain stories about satisfied customers and loyal employees rather than self-congratulatory statements by overpaid executives.

There are exceptions, of course, particularly in regulated industries where firms can get to be very profitable while serving customers poorly because they have a government granted monopoly. But ultimately, angry customers will find a way to break any abusive monopoly.

Watch for trends that change consumer behavior

Another way to find good long-term investments is to focus on sectors in the economy or industries that are likely to benefit from shifting consumer preferences or demographic change. An example of a shifting consumer preference is the demand for bigger homes. An example of a demographic trend is the extremely high growth of the Hispanic population.

The tricky part is not confusing fads and trends. Some fashion maven may declare, "Everyone will soon be wearing used clothing with holes in it." But this should not be interpreted as a trend. There must be some underlying reason, such as the shift to casual office dress, for a change in behavior by a few people to become a widespread trend.

The demand for bigger homes, for example, is fueled in large part by high growth in well-paid professional, executive, and managerial occupations where a big home is a status symbol as well as a place to entertain colleagues or clients.

The trend toward bigger homes is not just important for homebuilders. It's also beneficial to building-supply firms as well as home furnishings, landscaping, and interior-design companies. But as the population nearing retirement age grows ever larger, we may see a counter trend that will favor smaller custom-built homes.

Watch the money trends

One way to discover a trend is to think about how people spend the trillions of dollars that power the huge U.S. economy. Even a slight shift can mean a huge difference in demand for certain products or services.

Demand shifts when demographics change either in numbers of people or in wealth to spend. For example, the demographic segment of Hispanics is growing in numbers, while another segment, senior citizens, is growing in terms of affluence. In both cases, it's important to know that these populations are often geographically concentrated.

The growing number of Hispanics will mean a lot to businesses in states such as California, Texas, Florida, and New York, where there are large numbers of Hispanics. But that trend may not be of much consequence to local businesses in northern New England where few Hispanics reside.

In the case of seniors, or any other age group that is growing in numbers or wealth, think about what they buy more of than other households. For people aged 65 to 74, that includes travel, reading materials, and medical care. They are an important segment of the travel market, so if they have more cash, chances are they will spend more of it taking trips.

Consumer Trends for Investors

Over the next five years, the 11 percent growth rate of 55-to-64-year-olds is expected to double. The chart shows the trends in numbers of households and household income over the past five years for three important age groups and lists several areas where their spending is well above average. If their high rate of income growth keeps up and population growth accelerates, the top-spending categories may present investment opportunities.

CONSUMER SEGMENT TOP-SPENDING CATEGORIES	PAST FIVE-YEAR TREND

Ages 45 to 54:

| 21 million households | +19% |
| Average income: $72,000 | +22% |

Higher education, apparel, home furnishings, pets

Ages 55 to 64:

| 14 million households | + 11% |
| Average income: $61,000 | +28% |

Vacations, second homes, insurance, security systems

Ages 65 to 74:

| 11 million households | no change |
| Average income: $41,000 | + 33% |

Travel, reading, medical care, housekeeping services

Source: Bureau of Labor Statistics and Census Bureau

5 How to make sure your new business idea is sound

On any day, millions of Americans are thinking up new product and new business ideas. Those ideas plus the ability to carry them out make our economy not only the world's largest, but also the most vibrant and resilient.

In your enthusiasm for your new business ideas, don't forget to ask the basic questions needed to make sure the idea is viable. Many people do ask these kinds of questions. Here are two that the Marketing Advisor helped with.

Dear Marketing Advisor: I have two pet-related product ideas and have looked around to see if someone has already marketed them. So far, no one has, and rather than make them myself, I would like to sell my ideas. How do I go about approaching one or more companies without them stealing my ideas? **WS**

Dear WS: You have the classic inventor's problem. It is impossible to evaluate your idea unless you tell someone, but when you discuss the idea, you run the risk of losing it. There really is no perfect solution. If you are convinced that the idea has market potential, you may need to hire a lawyer who specializes in intellectual property law and have him or her write up a legal description of it and prepare a confidentiality agreement.

Then ask anyone with whom you wish to discuss your idea to sign the confidentiality agreement. The problem is that legal agreements cost money and you don't want to spend money on an idea that is simply not marketable. Remember the picture phone? Great idea, except that nobody wanted it.

One fairly quick way to determine the level of consumer interest in your products is to hire a market research firm to conduct one or two focus groups for you, with the firm and the participants signing your confidentiality agreement. But focus groups can cost $3,000 to $5,000 each. And you may not want to spend that much if there is only a small chance that your product can be successfully marketed.

The bottom line is that ideas are relatively easy to copy and as such are not as valuable as someone who can market them and develop them into a profitable business. You should be realistic about how much (or how little) you will get for the rights to any idea.

Dear Marketing Advisor: Could you give me an estimate for total purchases of lamps and lighting fixtures by U.S. households, particularly for households with $75,000 or more annual income and college-graduate-or-above level of education? **JR**

Dear JR: According to the lighting research firm, Market Studies, of Raleigh, NC (www.marketstudies.com), American households spent a total of $3.2 billion on lighting products last year. Household consumer expenditure surveys by the Bureau of Labor Statistics (www.bls.gov) provide a demographic profile of household spending for the category "lamps and other lighting fixtures."

So all the households in the U.S. above your $75,000 income threshold would be spending about $1.6 billion (half of the $3.2 billion national estimate by Market Studies) on lighting. Divide that by the number of U.S. households in that top income category (15.2 million according to the BLS) and the result is an average of $105 per high-income household spent on lighting per year.

Now get an estimate of $75,000+ income households in your market area (from the 2000 census or recent estimates) and multiply it by $105 and double the result. So if your market area has 20,000 such high-income households, a very rough estimate of the market potential for home lighting would be 20,000 times $105 times 2 or $4.2 million per year. Another product with a more complex demographic profile would of course require somewhat different calculations.

Big Spenders—Highest Spending
Households by Education and Income

College-graduate households spend 45 percent more in total than the average household, but spend only 28 percent more on food. They apparently save their money for reading and contributions. College-graduate households spend 55 percent more than average on reading material and contribute 124 percent more to various charities and non-profit organizations.

	COLLEGE GRADUATES	INCOME $70,000+	AVERAGE U.S. HOUSEHOLD
Weekly spending	$1,032	$1,477	$712
For food	124	167	97
For housing	342	444	232
For clothing	47	70	34

Source: Bureau of Labor Statistics

6 Now is the best time to bench-mark to your business location

How's business? In an uncertain economy, your answer may be: "It could be better." Well, if you know where your customers come from, now you can find out just how much better business could be. You can use census information to more accurately measure the sales potential in your trading area.

Measuring that sales potential creates a benchmark against which you can evaluate your business. It quantifies the maximum amount of business you could expect to get from your present location. You can later determine how much of that potential has in fact turned into sales for your business.

Benchmarking your business in this way enables you to answer the question: "Am I getting all the business I possibly can from this location?" If you are not, the next step is to think about what kind of changes you could make in your marketing or other parts of your operation to capture more of the potential business.

If your sales are approaching the total potential for your trading area, you are clearly doing something right because you have captured nearly all the possible business. In this situation, additional sales may come only from creating new ways to serve your existing customers, cultivating a new customer base, or looking for other locations.

Using demographics to benchmark

The 2000 census data are a critical part of creating a marketing benchmark because they provide up-to-date demographic information about potential customers. Here's the three- step process.

Step one: Go to the Census Bureau to find the demographic characteristics for any community in which you are doing or want to do business. The data are in the American FactFinder section of their web site (www.census.gov). The next two steps are up to you.

Step two: Find out which communities or neighborhoods generate most of your customers. In other words, define your trading area. If in the course of conducting business, you get your customers' names and addresses, then this is a simple matter. But if yours is a cash business, then it may be necessary to simply ask a sample of customers what community they come from or what zip code they live in.

Step three: Determine which of the residents of that trading area are most likely to become your customers and, if so, how much they are likely to spend. The more precise you can be about this the better. Suppose, for example, that nearly all your customers are homeowners. It is likely, however, that only certain homeowners will become regular customers. Finding that additional characteristic will make for a better benchmark.

The most common additional characteristic that businesses use is the age of the customer. The reason is that age is a fairly easy thing to observe or ask for, and many products are purchased more often at a certain stage of life. Paint and wallpaper, for example, are purchased by homeowners of all ages, but homeowners aged 55 to 64 spend 70 percent more than the average homeowner on those items.

Calculating the benchmark

Continuing with the above example, it's a good idea to make the first calculation using all homeowners and then refine it with age data. If your average customer spends, say, $400 a year and the census says that there are 12,000 homeowners, then the market potential may be as high as $4.8 million. But some homeowners will spend more than $400 a year and some will spend less.

Suppose the vast majority of your customers are older but not yet retired homeowners that you estimate are aged 45 to 64. Then your market potential may be smaller. Let's assume, for example, that in your trading area homeowners in that

American Homeowner Trends

The number of people in each home is shrinking, but the cost of ownership keeps rising.

	2000	1990	CHANGE 1990–2000
Owner-occupied housing units (millions)	69.8	59.0	+18%
Percent of all occupied units	66.2%	64.2%	+2%
Average number of persons in owned home	2.69	2.75	- 2%
Average annual spending on all home repairs	$560	$346	+ 62%

Source: 2000 Census & Bureau of Labor Statistics spending data

age group are only half of all homeowners. But they spend more: an average of $600 a year. Then your present sales potential is 6,000 times $600 or an estimated $3.6 million.

The comparison of that number to the larger figure for all homeowners suggests exploring what changes could be made to attract younger homeowners or retired ones.

These older and younger groups will probably not spend as much. But even if they only spent on average $200 a year, that would mean an additional 6,000 potential customers times $200 or $1.2 million of market potential, a one-third increase over your previous estimate.

Charting the benchmark

Benchmarking an existing business means evaluating the business in the context of the potential that exists in the trading area at this time. But that potential changes over time as people age or move away or as new people come into an area.

If, the number of potential customers in your trading area has grown 25 percent since the last census in 1990 and you were in business in 1990, has your business volume grown 25 percent or more since then? If not, you are not keeping pace with market growth. You may be giving up business to a competitor or just sustaining opportunity loss.

On the other hand, if the people most likely to become your customers are declining in numbers because they are moving away or getting older, then that may explain why sales have been slowing. In that case, searching for a new location or changing what your business offers may be strategies to consider.

Give yourself a marketing edge

7 It's hard, but make a plan for best results

Do you prefer to *do* anything rather than *write* something? If so, you're not alone. Most small-business owners are action-oriented folks who believe that success comes from hard work and long hours—not from writing plans. This attitude is understandable because writing is so often a solitary and mentally exhausting effort. It can seem much more productive, and more fun to just go out and sell something.

But there are several good reasons to consider planning before taking action. A plan can create accountability and save you from spending money on unproductive things like plush offices. A plan can assure that critical elements, however small, are not forgotten. And finally, a plan can help you focus your most precious resource—your time—where it will do the most good. We all waste some time, but a good plan can prevent wasting all of it.

Marketing is the one aspect of business where planning is crucial. Without a plan you will never know if your selling, advertising, or other marketing efforts are worth what they cost. And without a plan you won't have any benchmarks against which to measure the growth rate of your business. Here are a few suggestions for your next marketing plan.

Make a list

There are many ways to reach prospects and persuade them to buy something. List them all, from advertising to direct marketing to building a web site. It's easier to make a list than to write text describing what you are going to do. And you can always choose not to do something on your first list because it's too expensive or just not appropriate. But making a full list ensures that no useful marketing activity is forgotten.

Your list will change depending on whether your business is a start-up or well established. But no matter how old your business may be, there will always be new prospects that will need to be informed about who you are and what you offer, just as there are new ways to reach them, such as advertising on web sites or on the sides of trucks.

Almost all marketing lists include some form of direct marketing or selling in addition to advertising. This is because the results from direct marketing can be measured for each dollar spent. However, direct marketing alone may not be sufficient because over time any prospect list can become fatigued, causing a decline in response rates and sales. Besides, direct marketing works a lot better once you have established your brand identity.

Integrate your marketing for better results

Directly measurable marketing is always more effective when it is supported with advertising, or other marketing activities, the results of which may not be so easily measured. One important concept is called "integrated marketing," which is another way of describing carefully coordinated or blended marketing for better results.

Integrating or blending several marketing activities at once has been shown to be much more effective than just trying one or two elements. For example, think about any ad that you have seen recently on television or heard on the radio for a product or service you knew nothing about. Instead of being persuaded to buy the advertised item, you may have been thinking: "What is this and why should I care?"

But think how much more effective it would have been if prior to seeing or hearing the ad you had seen a print advertisement, or read a story about the company and its new product or service as a result of a press release. The chances are much greater that you will be more receptive to its selling proposition because you now have some idea of who the company is as well as an image in your mind of what it offers.

So when you make your list of possible marketing activi-

Advertising Spending Trends in Selected Media

Wilkofsky Gruen Associates forecast the growth rate of web site advertising to be double the average, but still far below the super high growth rates of the past.

MEDIUM	PROJECTED AD SPENDING	ANNUAL GROWTH RATE 2000–2004
Newspapers	$49.2 billion	+5.5%
Broadcast TV	$42.1	+5.7
Radio	$19.6	+7.6
Consumer magazines	$13.0	+6.5
Trade magazines	$11.2	+7.9
Internet web sites	$7.6	+16.1
Total six media listed	$142.7	+7.8

Source: Wilkofsky Gruen Associates

ties along with your cost and revenue expectations, consider also the timing of each effort so as to maximize the effectiveness of your total marketing budget. Trying one thing and then another will not be nearly as effective as doing several things in an integrated way.

Don't forget market research

In every industry, the marketing plans of the most successful companies discuss their plans for customer and consumer research. Your customers' wants or needs are certain to change, and when they do, you don't want to be the last to find out. An essential part of any marketing plan is an assessment of the market for what you plan to sell. This is a good place for another list—a list of questions for customers and prospects.

The bottom line

The most effective marketing plans are the ones where customers' needs are thought about first, where the author periodically rereads the plan to update it and measure the effectiveness of the overall marketing program, and where everyone involved has the patience to allow enough time for the advertising part of the plan to work.

8 How to begin marketing

A question I am often asked is, "How do I begin marketing if I want to start a business?" The exploratory phase of getting a business going always involves answering lots of questions about what you are providing and who is going to buy it. Since the last thing any business needs is nasty surprises, getting reasonably accurate answers before the business gets going can save you a lot of money and headaches later on.

Three marketing questions

From a marketing perspective, the three most important questions are about customers, competitors, and marketing expenses.

- Who are the customers likely to be and how many are there?
- Who are the competitors likely to be and how strong are they?
- How much will I have to spend on advertising, promotion, packaging, web sites, and other marketing to achieve the initial business objectives (or at least get enough revenue to be profitable)?

Finding out about customers is the first order of business, because if there are not enough customers willing to buy what you are selling, the time to find out is before you start the business. You would be surprised at the number of people who have told me that they intend to invest half a million dollars or more in a new business, but they don't have a couple of thousand dollars for some up-front market research.

The usual comment I hear from people averse to spending money on research is, "Well, all of my friends tell me that this is a great idea and that's all I need to know." This brings me to two of my marketing rules of thumb, which may help you in planning for the launch of your new firm.

Two marketing rules

Rule One states that your friends may be fine folks, but your future customers will probably not be like them, and in any case, it is unlikely that your friends are numerous enough or are willing to spend enough on a regular basis to sustain your business. Stated more bluntly: your friends are not likely to become your customers and your customers will almost certainly not be your friends or even people like them.

Rule Two states that for every dollar (of yours, the banks', or other people's money) you plan to invest in starting an enterprise, you should be prepared to spend up to two cents, or 2 percent of the total investment, on getting professional answers to the marketing questions above. Look at it this way. Even if you spend the whole 2 percent and find out that this business model won't work, you have saved 98 percent of your investment to use on another more viable idea.

One marketing plan

A marketing plan is essentially the document that contains the answers to the questions raised above. Taking the time to write down all the things you learn about customers, competitors, and marketing questions will not only impress any financial backers you might have, but it will also be useful once the business starts rolling. A pre-launch marketing plan also serves as an excellent benchmark from which you can measure your progress.

A big part of the plan should be a description of exactly who you expect to become customers and how much, on average, each of them is expected to spend. A description of the potential customers needs to be framed in terms of their demographic attributes, not in terms of their needs. Saying that your customers will be, for example, people who go out to dinner or people who buy expensive clothes won't help much when it comes to spending your marketing dollars wisely.

But saying that your prospective customers are, for example, couples with a household income over $50,000 a year, or professionally employed women, will enable you to get an estimate of how many are in the area you plan to serve and enable you to better focus your marketing efforts.

Most people want to start a business because they have some expertise in the product or service. For example, chefs who graduate from culinary school often start restaurants.

Small-Business Statistics

Contrary to popular belief, most small business start-ups do not fail.

Number of U.S. business starts annually .... 900,000 +

Percent started at home 60%

Ratio of start-ups to bankruptcies .... 20 to 1

Number of businesses filing tax returns .... 25 million

Ratio of tax-paying businesses to failures .... 345 to 1

Source: SBA

But it is rare for such people to also have the knowledge to develop a marketing plan for their businesses. In any case, most of the entrepreneurs I've met were in love with their business concepts and were hardly neutral when evaluating pre-launch research.

This is why I always recommend the use of a professional market research firm to provide an impartial evaluation of the demand for your product or service. By surveying potential customers or conducting focus groups, they can tell you a lot about how eager potential customers are to buy at the prices you want to charge.

9 Poll customers and prospects for valuable feedback

Mark your calendar! At least once every quarter, ask this question: "What have we learned about our customers or prospects in the past 90 days?" If the answer is, "Not much!" then perhaps you are missing some sales opportunities.

Learning about what customers or prospects think of your business is not an expensive undertaking, although that's often the excuse for not doing it. The real reason most firms do not regularly seek customer feedback is that they are afraid of the results. They take any negative comments personally. In a small firm, doing customer research is like asking people: "What do you think of me?" Few people really want to hear the answer.

So the first barrier to overcome is human nature. We don't take critical comments well. One way to get over it is to remember that firms who regularly solicit customer comments make a lot more money and stay in business a lot longer. Not convinced yet? Well, while reading these few tips for conducting customer research think about this: You are not a bad person just because someone doesn't like your product or service, but you might be losing a lot of money anyway.

Tie comments to the transaction

A person contacts a business establishment with two things: money and expectations. How often they spend that money with you depends greatly on how well you meet their expectations. And customer expectations can be measured with a survey.

It doesn't have to be a complicated survey, but it needs to have at least three key elements:

> 1. A sentence or two thanking the customer and asking for their opinions;
>
> 2. One or more questions relating to expectations or customer satisfaction, one or two questions asking if the customer would return or recommend the business; and
>
> 3. A space for comments.

For example, a hotel I stayed at recently gave me a list of the different services they offered (i.e., room service, wake-up call, business center, health club, etc.). Next to each was a row of boxes where I could check one of the following options: below expectations, met expectations, exceeded expectations, or somewhere in between. The last question before the comments section was: If you return to this area, would you stay here again?

It is important to survey customers very soon after their interaction with your business.

Surveys can be done by mail, over the phone, or on the web, but it is important to survey customers very soon after their interaction with your business. For some businesses like auto-repair services, collecting the customer's phone number is a normal part of the transaction. So calling customers within 24 hours of picking up their car may be efficient. Phoning them a week later may not yield much if they can't recall details of their visit.

Reward participation and make it short

Sadly, most surveys get thrown away or ignored because the would-be respondents do not see any immediate payoff in improving your business. This can be fixed by offering respondents something of value tied to their participation. You can offer a coupon for a future purchase or service. A benefit for you is that you get an address for future mailings, but that may discourage participation from people who prefer anonymity.

One way to increase participation even for those who want to be anonymous is to offer to make a donation to a local charity for every completed survey. Providing a short list from which to choose, including, for example, the United Way, the Red Cross, the Salvation Army, or a similar local non-profit service provider, may increase response even more.

Surveying customers is more art than science because it often involves balancing competing interests. Anonymous comments encourage people to respond candidly, but it is also nice to get a phone number or address for follow-up questions, to fix something for an unhappy customer, or to simply send a thank you note. At the end of the questionnaire, most firms let the customer choose whether to be contacted again.

Part of the art in surveying customers is knowing when to quit. You may want customers to tell you all their demographics, how they learned about you, and other things, in addition to how happy they are with your products or service. Resist the temptation to load up the questionnaire. A short survey will get you more respondents and better results than a long one that few people will complete. And you can always go back with another short survey to fill in any gaps in your customer knowledge.

Poll prospects

It is harder to get feedback from prospects than from customers, but you can get a big payoff from learning why they chose not to do business with you. Some of the reasons may be out of your control, but in most cases, there is some negative perception on the part of would-be customers that you can change—if you know what it is.

Prospects who encounter uninformed or aggressive sales people may just go away.

If customers contact you and then choose not to buy, you may be able to fix a problem in your operation or your marketing if you can find the reason why. For example, prospects who encounter uninformed or aggressive salespeople may just go away. Unless they tell you about such a problem, you might not be aware of how much business is going elsewhere.

One way to get prospect feedback is to do a phone survey of people who you think should be doing business with you and ask if they have ever contacted your firm. If they have, a few questions about why they went elsewhere should help you pinpoint the problem.

10 Things to think about before buying advice

Are you between a rock and a hard place? Are you worried about the direction your business is taking? In tough economic times, customers may start cutting back on their spending despite your best marketing efforts. That's when many business people think about hiring a marketing consultant.

The concept is to hire an experienced outsider who might have some ideas that you haven't thought of because you are too close to the problem and are probably worrying too much about it. If your revenues are starting to wither, hiring a marketing consultant may seem like a reasonable course of action, but you'll be much happier with the result if you accurately define the problem and manage your expectations.

What's the real problem?

When sales are dropping, the problem may not be in your marketing efforts but somewhere else. There is a reason management consultants outnumber marketing consultants three to one. The problem is far more likely to be in management than marketing.

Dilbert is an extremely popular cartoon because it portrays examples of outrageously bad management with which many of us are, unfortunately, familiar. But in a small business, management is not some distant bureaucracy; it's you. That's why the first step in solving a marketing problem is to discover what or who is the problem.

The trick to doing that is to take some time to talk to your employees as well as some past or present customers. If that is not possible, at least review any results from past customer research. Then define what you think is the real problem and write it down.

Avoid the trap of just thinking that if you spent more money promoting your business, everything would be okay. If there are problems with your product, your service, or the management of your business, those problems have to be addressed before trying to attract more customers who may, after an initial inquiry, not buy anything.

A common problem among start-ups today is that customers buy something once and don't return.

Define your expectations

After you have defined what you think the problem is, add to it what you expect your consultant to do about it. This is a critical piece. David Stone, a marketing consultant since 1986 and partner in the New England Consulting Group in Westport, CT, says: "One of the difficulties we have is being hired to find a solution to the wrong problem."

Stone believes that prospective clients should not expect an immediate "grand solution," but should expect to spend quite a bit of time with their consultant defining the work plan, the timetable, and a specific deliverable. He also thinks that clients should expect their consultants to "challenge management's view of the business."

A common problem among start-ups today is that customers buy something once and don't return. The result is rev-

Businesses That Sharpen Your Marketing Edge

There are over 50,000 firms in the U.S. that provide marketing related services. They employ over 600,000 people, but most are small firms averaging only 11 employees each.

BUSINESS TYPE	# OF U.S. FIRMS	WITH <10 EMPLOYEES	AVERAGE SALARY
Marketing consultants	13,500	92%	$52,400
Ad agencies	13,600	80	$57,600
Other ad services	9,500	88	$29,400
Public-relations firms	6,600	87	$55,900
Direct-marketing firms	4,300	64	$31,100
Marketing-research firms	4,200	60	$29,100

Source: Census Bureau

enue shortfall despite big marketing expenses. The situation may be due to a number of factors including poor product quality or customer service or that the customers you are attracting have only a limited need for what you're selling. A good marketing consultant will have an open mind about the causes as well as the full range of solutions.

Expect the unexpected

The maximum benefit of hiring consultants will come when they see something you can't see. It's not that you don't have vision; it's just that they often see things differently. However, this will only occur when they have all the facts and free range to explore all aspects of your business.

The standard joke is that consultants take your watch and then tell you what time it is. And if they're really good, they keep the watch. Like all good business jokes, that one resonates because consultants sometimes report what you already knew. You will probably be disappointed if that happens.

You can avoid disappointment by being very specific about what you expect from the consultants you interview. Be alert for prepackaged solutions, preconceived notions, or uninformed speculation about your business problem. When reading proposals look for indications that, while the consultants may have experience with similar situations, they have an open mind and intend to help you find a fact-based and realistic solution to your problem.

11 What can we learn from the dot-com disasters?

There is always something to be learned from someone else's misfortune. That's why people tend to drive more carefully after seeing a car upside down in a ditch. Well, unfortunately there are a lot of internet firms with their wheels in the air, and their sad end has something to teach those of us who have, so far, avoided catastrophe.

Reading the short history of some of these firms reminds the rest of us that, despite having high-tech wizardry, there is still no substitute for common sense when communicating with customers. Here are three marketing-related departures from common sense that can prove fatal to any business, whether it's on the internet or not.

1. Field of dreams marketing The white-hot excitement of starting a "new economy" business can easily cloud normally good judgment. Entrepreneurs who are passionate about their start-ups almost always believe the field of dreams myth that if you build something big, customers will magically appear. So, unfortunately, many felt no need (or thought they had no time) to conduct any serious research to determine the extent of the actual demand for what they wanted to sell, and how that demand was being satisfied.

Measuring demand is complicated by the fact that most consumers are pretty satisfied with the firms they currently use and are reluctant to change, particularly if there is any perceived risk. People who start businesses are certainly risk takers and often have difficulty understanding that ordinary consumers are really quite risk averse, particularly when the transaction is conducted in the new and unruly world of cyberspace.

In some new-economy start-ups the strategy appeared to be advertise first and figure out the business fundamentals later. Too often, the e-commerce firms ig-

Ordinary consumers are really quite risk averse.

nored basic customer needs, such as on-time delivery and adequate customer support in favor of flashy web sites and lots of expensive advertising.

2. Spending big money on bad advertising According to the Electronic Retailing Association, dot-com companies spent $7 billion on advertising in 2000 to bring in about $300 million in revenue. You do not need a degree in business management to know that meant spending over $20 on advertising to create $1 worth of business. By that measure their advertising wasn't just bad—it was dreadful. At a bare minimum, any business should expect to get back more revenue than the amount spent on advertising.

Bad advertising in this context means advertising that may have been fun to look at or even won awards, but it did not work—it didn't sell the product or even build a brand. The sad part about that wasted $7 billion is that it was so avoidable. All they had to do was test the advertising before buying expensive TV time.

There is a substantial industry made up of firms that pre-test advertising for effectiveness. They even have their own industry association in New York City called the Advertising

Research Foundation. The bottom line is that there is no excuse for spending money on advertising that produces so little revenue.

3. Mistaking your habits for consumer behavior Many of the dot-com companies were started and staffed by highly educated young people with a great deal of computer expertise and passion for using cutting-edge software. They were also used to having very fast computers and high-speed internet connections. Their marketing messages and complex websites seemed to be designed for people like themselves, despite the fact that only a tiny fraction of Americans fit that profile.

A fairly common marketing mistake made by business managers is thinking that everyone lives like they do or

Internet Audience Numbers

Despite billions of dollars spent on dot-com advertising in 2000, only about half of U.S. households had internet access and only 38 percent reported using it at home in the prior month. By contrast 90 percent of American households have a VCR and more than two-thirds have cable TV and read a Sunday newspaper.

	NUMBER	PERCENT OF TOTAL
Total U.S. adults	200.6 million	100.0%
With any internet usage	99.4	49.6
Have access at home	88.7	44.2
Used last month	75.4	37.6
Have access at work	56.2	28.0
Used last month	45.6	22.7

Note: Used last month means used in last 30 days.
Source: Mediamark Research, Inc.

shares their passion for what they make. You may love to play golf, but your customers might prefer to go bowling. You may be able to instantly bring up flashing graphic images with your cable modem, while your customers could be struggling with a painfully slow dial-up telephone connection.

The consequences of not taking the time to understand how your customers' situation and preferences are different from yours are pretty straightforward. Your customers probably will not understand what you are talking about, and your marketing won't sell nearly as much as you think it should.

A common mistake made by business managers is thinking that everyone lives like they do.

It's a shame that so many talented people had to lose their companies and their jobs to remind us that, in the rush of doing business, we should not depart from common sense of learning something about our customers before we start doing the talking.

12 Cutting costs may foreclose future business

Whenever the stock market declines or the dreaded recession word is mentioned, across the land, you can almost hear that awful sound of wallets slamming shut. Since we now have all news all the time, it is only a matter of minutes before every business gets the message—the economy is going down for the count; better count your cash and cut back on spending. And what's the quickest way to cut your business expenses? Slash the marketing budget, of course.

After every economic downturn for the past 30 years, studies have shown what a big mistake it is to chop the one budget item that keeps new and existing customers coming in. Every such study shows the same thing. Businesses that stop or sharply curtail marketing suffer a lot more from bad economic times than those who maintain regular communication with their customers.

This is not to say that throwing money at silly ads is ever a good idea. Spending money on poorly performing advertising is a dumb idea no matter how rosy the economy outlook. But when consumer spending slows, it is just good common sense to keep talking to your core customer base and make sure they know you're still very much in business.

While maintaining an appropriate level of marketing, messages need to be altered so that they stay in harmony with consumers' changing state of mind. Shifts in economic activity are partly driven by changes in consumer attitudes. When a decline in the index of consumer confidence is reported, many consumers read about it and to no one's surprise, their confidence in the future may be weakened and they tend to spend less freely.

The best advertising during a slowing economy acknowledges that consumers are likely to be nervous about spending money and more careful with their purchases. They may need some assurance from your advertising that spending money with you is still a good idea.

When consumer confidence is waning, a perception of enduring value can make the difference between a sale and no sale.

Here are some guidelines for customer communication in troubled economic times.

Stress the attribute of lasting value. Since most consumers are normally risk averse, product or service attributes like guarantees and durability are almost always useful advertising themes. But when consumer confidence is waning, a perception of enduring value can make the difference between a sale and no sale.

When stock prices decline, financial commentators often talk about "the flight to quality." What they mean is that, in uncertain times, investors tend to buy more stock in what they know to be financially sound companies. Likewise in uncertain times, consumers are more likely to buy from firms they think will survive and avoid firms they think are shaky.

Without being obvious, advertising when the economy is weak should stress financial strength and stability over humorous themes or deep discounts. One way to do this is to get testimonials from large or long-time customers in which they talk about how happy they have been with your service over the many years they have done business with you.

One theme that works particularly well to encourage return business is safety. The idea is to remind customers that there is no need to take a chance with someone new when they can just return to you. But this assumes that their experience with you was a positive one, which may or may not have been the case.

Take good care of your regular customers. In an overheated economy like we experienced in 2000, regular customers often get taken for granted. That's unfortunate, because when business softens, it's those dependable spenders who can sustain your business, provided you haven't been ignoring them. Many of the now deceased dot-coms forgot that customer service is a crucial part of marketing.

A major purpose of consistent advertising is to give existing customers a reason to return and remind them why they made such a smart choice in doing business with you in the first place. When the business climate turns cold, marketing messages that tell existing customers how much you appreciate them really pay off.

Advertising themes like safety, quality, or enduring value always work better when they are backed up by a little market research. Something to be avoided is advertising a benefit or attribute that is not credible, particularly to your existing customers. Better to find out with research why your regular customers keep returning than to guess and be wrong.

III

Trends for the new millennium

13 Census figures show a fast-changing America

It wasn't that long ago that the Census Bureau was tabulating questionnaires. But now we have the numbers on how the country has changed over the past ten years in terms of age, household type, and family relationships. Here's the story, and the facts.

Household change

Households total 105.5 million, up 14.7 percent from the 1990 count of about 92 million. Every week during the 1990s, 26,000 new households were formed, each of which needed furniture, appliances, curtains, and the hundreds of other things that make a house a home.

As in past decades, households grew faster than population, but only slightly. Total population was up 13.2 percent. This means that the average number of people living in each household continues to drop. It is now 2.59, compared with 2.63 in 1990. One of the most interesting consumer contradictions is that as the number of people in each household declines, the average size of new dwelling units increases—up about 7 percent since 1990.

Homeownership rates continue to grow. There are now about 70 million homeowners in the U.S., two-thirds of all households, up 18 percent or 10.7 million units since 1990.

Top & Bottom U.S. Counties

Largest U.S. county:	Los Angeles, CA	9.5 million people
Smallest U.S. county:	Loving, TX	67 people
Fastest growth county since 1990:	Douglas, TX	up 191%
Slowest growth county:	Aleutian Islands, AK	down 42%

Source: 2000 census

Renter-occupied units edged up only 2 percent. That may explain why there is such a shortage of affordable rental housing for people who are not able to buy a house.

The fastest-growing families during the past decade were those headed by single moms, up 25 percent. In the parlance of the Census Bureau, there were 7.6 million "female householders, no husband present, with own children under 18," an increase of 1.5 million since 1990. By contrast, "married couples with own children under 18" edged up 5.7 percent since 1990 to 24.8 million, an increase of just 1.3 million. Only 24 percent of households are married couples with children.

Married couples without children grew 9 percent, but non-family households jumped 23 percent. Non-families are people who live alone or with other people to whom they are not related. People who live alone increased 21 percent to 27.2 million, one in every four households. But people who cohabitate jumped 33 percent to 6.5 million households. While the number of cohabitators may be growing fast, they are still only about 6 percent of all households.

Changing age structure

It's well known that we are all getting older, but here are some details. Half of all Americans are now over 35 years old. Twenty years ago, the median age was only 30.

The largest age group in 1990 was 25-to-34-year-olds, to-day it's 35 to 44, and in 2010 it will be 45 to 54. By contrast, the largest age group in Mexico is under 10 years old.

The fastest-growing age group during the past decade was 45-to-54-year-olds—up 49 percent. So during this decade, the fastest-growing age group will be people aged 55 to 64. The population of young adults aged 25 to 34 actually de-

Changing U.S. Age Structure

AGE GROUP	CENSUS COUNT (millions)	PERCENT CHANGE 1990-2000
Under 5	19.2	+4.5%
5 to 14	41.1	+16.7
15 to 24	39.2	+6.6
25 to 34	39.9	-7.6
BABY BOOM		
35 to 44	45.1	+20.1
45 to 54	37.7	+49.4
55 to 64	24.3	+14.8
65 to 74	18.4	+1.6
75 to 84	12.3	+22.9
85 or older	4.2	+37.6
Total	281.4	+13.2

Source: Census Bureau, 2000 census

Are you above average?

All figures are March 2000 except income, which is 1999.

Average age of U.S. women .... 37 years, 8 months
Average age of U.S. men .... 35 years, 2 months

Average household income (under age 65) $60,129
When householder is college graduate $88,184

Average number of persons per household 2.59
Average number of earners per household 1.42

Average married couples' annual income $70,880
When both work full time $87,482

Percent of all married couples
  who have no children at home 52%

Source: U.S. Census Bureau

clined a bit, which may explain some of the labor shortages in the service industries.

Look out! The teenage population is growing again. Ten- to-14-year-olds are up 20 percent since 1990, which means more teenagers should be hitting the malls right about now. Colleges should be happy because a new baby boom will be graduating from high school over the next decade. Their parents will probably spend a fortune sending them off to college.

There are 41 million children aged 5 to 14 and another 39 million aged 15 to 24. That's almost as many as the original baby boomers, which according to the Census Bureau, are now about 83 million people aged 35 to 54. Just as the first baby boom moves into its retirement years, the

U.S. Demographics Diversify

Since 1990 the number of Americans who identify themselves with
one or more racial or ethnic groups has increased dramatically.
Approximately one in three of the all racial or ethnic minorities is
under age 18. Fewer than one in four census respondents
identified as white, not Hispanic, are under age 18.

	CENSUS COUNT	CHANGE 1990–2000	UNDER AGE 18
Total U.S. population	281.4 million	+13.2%	26%
White, not Hispanic	194.6	+ 3.4	23
Hispanic or Latino	35.3	+57.9	35
Black or African American	34.7	+15.6	31
Black, not Hispanic	33.9	+16.2	31
Asian, not Hispanic	10.1	+52.4	24
Other race, not Hispanic	2.9	+22.0	34
Multi-racial, not Hispanic	4.6	+87.8	41

Source: Census Bureau

next baby boom will be ready to take its place in the
workforce.

Speaking of retirees, the census revealed an almost
complete lack of growth among 65-to-74-year-olds. This
age group only grew 1.6 percent since 1990. Older Americans increased more rapidly, however, with 75-to-84-year-
olds up 23 percent and those aged 85 or older up 38 percent to 4.2 million.

The ratio of people aged 65 or older to those aged 18 to
64 is now one to five, slightly higher than in 1990.

The number of children increased 14 percent since 1990, much better than during the 1980s when there was no change at all. Because there are more male births, boys slightly outnumber girls. Among 72 million children under age 18, there are about 1.8 million more boys than girls. But after age 18 the ratio flips. From age 18 to 64, there are about 1 million more women than men.

Of all people aged 65 or older, there are 6 million more women than men. The number of men is increasing somewhat faster than women, partly because of heavy immigration, which tends to be mostly men, but also because men are living longer. The number of men aged 65 and older increased 15 percent since 1990, versus only a 10 percent increase for women in the same age group.

14 Education often predicts consumer behavior

Every year, more high school graduates go on to college and more college graduates go back for an advanced degree. A recent Census Bureau survey found that one in four U.S. adults aged 25 or older has either a bachelor's or advanced degree. Fifteen years ago, that figure was fewer than one in five.

This rising level of educational attainment is important to anyone marketing consumer goods because advanced education often changes consumer behavior and alters product preferences. For one thing, college graduates are almost all familiar with the internet and use it frequently to find information about a product or service.

One of the more interesting trends in higher education is that college graduates tend to marry other college graduates, and in most cases both spouses continue their careers. This can create households with very high income but little free time. The Census Bureau reports that the 27 percent of households headed by college graduates take home nearly half (42 percent) of all aggregate household income.

But just knowing household income is not as useful for marketing purposes as it used to be. The value of income as a predictor of consumer behavior is diminishing due in part to growing privacy concerns and consequent reluctance by consumers to reveal how much money they make. However,

Growth in Well-Educated Consumers

EDUCATIONAL ATTAINMENT	CHANGE 1990 TO 2000
High school graduates	+ 10%
Some college or associates degree	+ 21
Bachelor's degree	+ 37
Graduate degree	+ 39
All persons aged 25+	+ 12

Source: Census Bureau

most people will readily tell you where they went to community college, university, or graduate school, and what level of education they attained.

Insights into how education changes consumer behavior can be found in many studies, but one of the most cited is the Consumer Expenditure Survey by the Bureau of Labor Statistics. The survey reports that the average U.S. household spends about $37,000 a year on all goods and services. But households headed by someone with a bachelor's degree spend about $50,000 a year, and those with advanced degrees spend over $60,000.

So a household with higher education spends, on average, between $135 and $164 for every $100 that an average household spends for all goods or services. However, that difference widens for some products or services and disappears for others.

Households with higher education, for example, spend less than the average household for some kinds of food (meat, sugar), but about 1.4 times as much for fresh fruits, vegetables, and fresh fish. People with advanced degrees are far more likely to be vegetarians than the average adult. This is of consequence if food is served at a marketing event targeted at this segment.

When it comes to alcoholic beverages, households with advanced degrees also spend less than average on beer, but three times as much on wine. When marketing to highly educated consumers, a fine bottle of wine is a much sought-after premium. For event marketing, a wine-tasting session will probably be more attractive to this type of customer than a barbecue.

Perhaps the place where college graduates really spare no expense is on their homes. They spend 1.7 times the average for all home expenses, but more than twice as much for housekeeping services, lawn care, and outdoor furniture.

For some reason, education and plants seem to go together. Householders with advanced degrees spend the most of any household type on indoor plants and fresh flowers— $220 for every $100 that the average household spends.

When it comes to furniture, appliances and housewares as well as clothes, more highly educated households don't necessarily buy more of them. They just buy more expensive designer items and items of better perceived quality. The attributes of uniqueness and visual attractiveness are probably more important than price.

Any business that wants to attract well-educated customers would be well advised to decorate its premises with live plants and fresh flowers. Hyatt Hotels figured this out years ago and their usually crowded lobbies are virtual jungles.

People with higher education also travel more for both business and pleasure. So they naturally spend more on luggage, cell phones, and laptop computers. And they spend nearly three times the average household on software.

One of the interesting attributes of highly educated people is they never seem to get enough of it. Households headed by college graduates spend more than twice the average household for all kinds of educational products and services as well as books, newspapers, and magazines. It seems that once people see the value of acquired knowledge, they want more of it.

College graduates spend more than twice the average for house-keeping services, lawn care, and outdoor furniture.

The marketing implications are clear. If you wish to attract more highly educated customers, make sure that there is heavy information content in your marketing materials and stress the values of high-quality, design, and uniqueness. And don't forget the flowers.

15 Household income is rising, but so are expenses

Does your household's total income exceed $800 a week? If so, you can say that you are above average because more than half of the 105 million American households make less than you do. The Census 2000 Supplementary Survey found that exactly half of U.S. households lived on an annual income equal to or less than $41,343 ($795 a week) and the other half had more to spend.

During the 1990s, median income increased 38 percent from the $30,056 recorded in the 1990 census. But of course, nearly everything cost less in 1990, so if that thirty grand is adjusted for what it would actually buy today, it becomes $40,530. Therefore, in terms of real purchasing power, the U.S. median household income has edged up just 2 percent in the past ten years. But simply dividing the income scale into two equal parts doesn't properly account for all the increased wealth we have observed over the past decade.

What the income median does not show is that, between 1990 and 2000, the proportion of households making over $75,000 a year doubled from one household in ten to more than one household in five. At least part of the increase can be attributed to the presence of two or more high earners in the household. The bottom line is that this top fifth of the consumer income distribution is now the recipient of half of

2000 Census Comparisons for Selected States

The small state of New Hampshire has a higher median household income and faster income growth than some of the largest states in the nation.

STATE	INCOME	PERCENT CHANGE 1990–2000	PERCENT WITH MEDIAN INCOME $75,000+
California	$46,500	+30%	28%
Massachusetts	$49,505	+34	31
New Hampshire	$49,509	+36	27
New York	$43,640	+32	26
All 50 states	$41,343	+38	22

Source: Census 2000 Supplementary Survey

the more than $5 trillion earned or otherwise obtained annually by U.S. households.

Where the money goes

What have they done with all that money? Well, besides stocks and bonds, many households have bought bigger houses, more second homes, and more cars, trucks or SUVs. The number of homes with nine rooms or more, for example, has increased 25 percent since 1990, nearly twice the rate of growth for all housing units.

Homeownership has reached an all-time high, with two-thirds of householders owning their home. There are 10.8 million more owner-occupied homes in the U.S. today than in 1990, an 18 percent increase. The median value of homes is up 53 percent, but the number of owned homes valued at $500,000 or more jumped 150 percent in the past decade.

The odd thing about the increasing size and value of homes is that fewer people are living in each one. The 2000 census found the average number of people per household reached an all-time low of 2.59 people in each unit, down from 2.63 in 1990. There are more householders in America who live alone (27.2 million) than married couples with children (24.8 million). And there are more married couples with no children (29.6 million) than with them. So a majority of these bigger homes have only one or two people in them.

Households may have fewer people in them, but they have more vehicles than ever before. A majority of homes have two or more and 19.2 million households own three or more cars, trucks, or other means of personal transport. Perhaps because they have so many vehicles, more than three out of four commuters drive to work alone.

What all this means, of course, is that some U.S. households are spending more and more of their increasing income on their homes. According to the Bureau of Labor Statistics (BLS), homeowners are paying 95 percent more in property taxes than they did ten years ago. And they are shelling out 60 percent more for maintenance, repairs, insurance, and other such homeowner expenses.

When the BLS adds it up, the average U.S. household spends nearly half (47 percent) of its after-tax income on its homes and cars. But if you are among the top one-fifth of households earning $75,000 a year or more, then you are only spending 35 percent of your income for housing and transportation.

For providers of other consumer goods and services, the message is clear. For many businesses, at least half of your sales, and probably a lot more, will come from the 20 percent of households with the most disposable income. Understanding how that segment of most-likely customers can be reached with a marketing message and how their need for household or other products and services is changing may be crucial to your future.

The odd thing about the increasing size and value of homes is that fewer people are living in each one.

This is so because, despite rising incomes for some, most households are spending large fractions of their income on the fairly fixed expenses of owning and maintaining their homes and vehicles. For those consumers, there will be increasing pressure to find less expensive goods and services or to delay or forego the purchase of non-essential items.

For more information on the household income trends for your state, check out the Census Bureau's website **www.census.gov** and look for the Census 2000 Supplementary Survey.

16 Rising consumer spending is sometimes marketing driven

Are you spending more for shoes, telephones, drugs and cable TV? Well, you are not alone. American households are shifting the money they spend on both the necessary and the not-so-necessary goods and services they buy. While personal spending is rising fast for some items like prescription drugs, spending on clothing is growing much more slowly.

Just because we spend more for something does not necessarily mean we buy more of it. Often, we are just paying more and sometimes we pay more because we want to. That's testimony to the power of marketing. Some households now pay more than twice as much for coffee as they used to because they now buy bags of imported beans from a coffee shop instead of buying it less expensively in a can from the supermarket.

Sometimes changes in lifestyles alter spending habits. Overall spending on furniture, for example, has increased only 19 percent between 1995 and 2000, according to the Bureau of Labor Statistics. But spending on outdoor furniture is up 41 percent as people cook and entertain more on their patios or decks.

Sometimes demographic change, such as an aging population, can alter spending. Overall spending on pets, for example, is up only 5 percent since 1995. However, being a veterinarian over the next decade should be a rewarding profession because the fast rising households headed by persons aged 55 to 64 have increased their overall spending for pets by 20 percent and added more than 37 percent to their vet bills since 1995. Pet groomers should do well, too.

Technology can play a part

From 1995 to 2000 overall spending for home-telephone service rose only 11 percent, but spending for mobile telephone service more than tripled. Was that a technology change or a lifestyle change? Perhaps a little of both. If the new cell phones with screens for surfing the internet become popular, perhaps spending on cell phone service will rise even faster. It may depend on whether they are marketed as just a cool toy or as an absolutely necessary personal communication tool.

Sometimes we pay more because we want to. That's testimony to the power of marketing.

Some services almost market themselves

It's well known that more highly educated people make more money, so it probably shouldn't be a surprise that spending on education has increased 34 percent (1995-2000). But perhaps much of that rise was just an increase in tuition, because spending on books (which are often discounted) was up only 7 percent.

Americans now spend more than four times as much on tuition than on heavily marketed pet food. Given the rapid increase in education spending and the entry of for-profit firms into a previously non-profit industry, we may see more

Spending Trends 1995 to 2000

CATEGORY	PERCENT CHANGE IN HOUSEHOLD SPENDING
Cable TV	+46%
Sound equipment	- 2
Computers & software (home use)	+34
Sports & exercise equipment	+30
Household decorative items	+29
Average all spending	+18%

Source: Bureau of Labor Statistics

sophisticated marketing for courses to make you smarter and perhaps even somewhat wealthier.

Education is also starting earlier. Spending on child-care centers, nursery schools, and pre-schools is up 43 percent, while spending for child care in someone's home has declined. Some of that shrinkage may be due to a growing reluctance to admit off-the-books nanny hiring, but there is no doubt that pre-school educational services are expanding.

Sometimes no amount of marketing can make up for a receding demand for a product or service. Between 1995 and 2000, spending for life insurance edged up only 4 percent, while personal contributions to retirement plans jumped 25 percent. It's been clear for some time that Americans generally have less fear of dying too soon than of living too long.

A longer-lived population will probably need more medical care and prescription drugs. But because health insurance plans usually cover services, personal expenditures for medical services are up only 11 percent (1995 to 2000).

Spending for prescription medicine, on the other hand, is up 52 percent, perhaps because pharmaceutical companies advertise directly to consumers.

It's well known that people are eating out more often. But now we have the facts. Despite having bigger and more expensive kitchens than ever before, American households spent only 8 percent more for food at home in 2000 than in 1995. But they spent 26 percent more eating out. At those differential growth rates, by the end of this decade, Americans will be spending more than half of their food budget eating out. (It's now 41 percent.)

Speaking of necessary spending, household clothing expenses are rising slowly, despite increased use of higher-priced designer labels. Discounting is so rampant in apparel that spending from 1995 to 2000 edged up only 5 percent for men's and 9 percent for women's clothing. Marketing must work better and mark-downs must be fewer on footwear, because spending is up 24 percent for men's shoes and up 32 percent for women's shoes in the same period.

Whatever consumer business you are in, the Bureau of Labor Statistics probably has some spending data relevant to your product or service. The data can be found at **www.bls.gov/cex/home.htm.**

17 Young house- holders are special customers

Stage of life is a strong predictor of what types of goods and services consumers will buy. Each age segment or life stage has a unique set of wants and needs, and that determines to a great extent how they spend money. As a result, the more you know about each age group, the sharper your marketing advantage.

The transition from one life stage to another is particularly important. For example, when a young person leaves his or her parents' home and finds a place to live, a new household is formed and a lifetime of purchasing things for that household begins. At first, the furnishings can often be described as early garage sale, but gradually, the junky stuff gets thrown out and is replaced with newer things, particularly after a wedding.

Marriage does not happen as early in life as it used to, but it's still an occasion for some big spending. Since most Americans form their first household and usually get married by their early 30s, here are some facts about the demographics and spending patterns of young-adult households.

Young households buy lots of kid stuff

People under age 35 account for about one out of every four households, but the most stable of those households are headed by persons aged 25 to 34. Fewer than 10 percent of U.S. householders are under age 25, and only a small fraction of those are either married or own their home. But the median age of first marriage is now 25 years. So more than one-half of the households aged 25 to 34 are married couples, and about one-half have become first-time homebuyers.

Household income increases in this age segment as well because nearly one-third of 25-to-34-year-olds have completed college or graduate school, and a majority have some college education. The median household income of all households in the 25-to-34 age category is over $42,000 a year. But for college graduates in that age group, annual household income exceeds $50,000.

Three-quarters of all U.S. births occur when the mother is aged 20 to 34.

Since three-quarters of all U.S. births occur when the mother is aged 20 to 34, a substantial portion of household income in that age bracket is devoted to buying goods and services for very young children. For example, the average two-earner household in the 25-to-34 age category with preschool children spends more for child care than for food. And families who can't get hand-me-downs spend over $1,000 a year on kids' clothes, according to the Bureau of Labor Statistics' household surveys.

The household food budget for the average 25-to-34-year-old is almost evenly split between at-home meals and restaurant or carry-out meals. No other household type spends more at fast-food restaurants. But their liquor and wine spending is way below average.

According to BLS surveys, these young households also spend much less than older households on lawn-and-garden stuff and less on products that are used to keep your house

Living Arrangements of 25-to-34-year-old Americans

Among those adults aged 25 to 34 who live with parents, men outnumber women two to one.

STATUS	MEN	WOMEN
Married	50%	57%
Living alone	12	8
Living with parents	12	6
Other arrangements*	26	29
Total	100%	100%

* Includes living with roommates or partners

Source: Census Bureau

clean. That makes sense—not many parents of small children have any spare time or energy to garden or clean the house.

Many couples in the 25-to-34 age group are forming households for the first time. It is a time when they are likely to develop long-term brand preferences for household products and services. As a result, they are flooded with advertising messages. A carefully targeted marketing message that speaks directly to their needs will almost certainly be more effective at reaching them in their busy lives than any general purpose advertisement.

Time is, of course, the major constraint on young families, particularly those with two earners and small kids. Any business that serves this market segment needs to be mindful of that and think about ways to minimize the time required to conduct business. Delivery services are very popular in this market segment.

Since most households in this market segment have an internet connection, providing quick access to detailed information on a web site about what your business offers and accepting e-mail inquiries can be an important marketing tool. Another useful marketing tool for this market segment is sponsorships or affinity marketing.

When developing marketing messages for this segment it's a good idea to keep their interests in mind. Their youth makes them more interested than older consumers in fashion, participation sports, and entertainment, but they are also interested in anything educational that might help them get better jobs or advance in their careers.

18 Young boomers are big spenders

Fortunes have been made by entrepreneurs who pay close attention to the wants and needs of baby boomers. The youngest of these legendary consumers are now in their mid-30s. In fact, the 2000 census reported the biggest ten-year age group in the U.S. is boomers aged 35 to 44.

Every week, the 24 million households in that age bracket spend over $20 billion nationwide on consumer goods and services. For local businesses that cover a typical residential zip code with 5,000 homes, this age group alone could be worth thousands of dollars a week.

What do we know about these youngest baby boomers? Well, most of them are married with children and own their home. Six out of ten households are married couples and two-thirds of the households in this age bracket have children. More than two-thirds of the families are also homeowners, so a large portion of their above-average income is spent on their kids or on their house.

Average annual household income for 35-to-44-year-old baby-boomer households exceeds $60,000, and one in six households in this age group earns over $100,000 a year, according to the Census Bureau. One reason for the above-average income is that the vast majority of married couple households in this age bracket have two earners.

But if they have teenage kids, chances are they have multiple spenders as well.

Boomers spend the most on food

No other age group spends more on food because no other group has so many mouths to feed. One-half of the families in the 35-to-44 age category have two or more children. So we should not be surprised that nobody spends more on cereal, cookies, dairy products, frozen foods, or potato chips.

Despite spending 21 percent more than the average household on food at home, these boomers also spend 24 percent more than average on food away from home. More than one-third (35 percent) of their total food budget is spent eating out. If you own a "family" restaurant, this age group will probably account for between one-fourth and one-third of your revenue.

Since many restaurants serve wine and beer, it's interesting to note that total spending on alcoholic beverages peaks in this age group. But when buying something to drink at home, 35-to-44-year-olds appear to be shifting some of their spending from beer to wine. The young boomer households that buy wine spend an average of about $20 a week, according to the Bureau of Labor Statistics.

Big house spenders

Housing costs consume about one-third of most households' income. And since householders aged 35 to 44 have the biggest families of any age group, they need more space. More space requires more furnishings as well as more energy for lighting, heating, cooling, and appliances.

But when you buy a big house, the monthly mortgage payments, property taxes, and insurance don't leave much for expensive home furnishings. For younger homeowners, particularly those with children, low-cost furniture is a must. So there would seem to be a substantial opportunity for a provider of used or refurbished tables, chairs, sofas, and other common household items.

Households in this age group, however, spend a lot for computers and internet access for themselves and their children. The average wired household in the 35-to-44 age category spends more each year on computer-related expenses than all other home appliances combined. Computer repair and maintenance alone for this age group is nearly a $100 million-a-year business.

Other spending balances out

Any household group that spends so much on their kids and their home is bound to spend less on some other things. Young boomers spend less than many other age groups on adult clothing but spend the most of any household age segment on clothing for children aged 2 to 15. They also spend less than average on jewelry.

Despite the allure of buying new cars, on average, young boomers are more than twice as likely to buy a used, rather than a new, car or truck. That bodes well for local repair shops whose job it is to keep those older cars running. Men in this age group rarely buy motorcycles, probably so their teenage kids won't get any ideas.

Because they are still relatively young, households aged 35 to 44 spend much less than average on medical expenses

Young-Boomer Trends—Aged 35 to 44

Median household income $50,900

Increase in median since 1995 .... +17%

Number of $100,000+ income households .... 3.5 million

Increase in such households since 1995 .... +78%

Change since 1995 in all household spending........................ +12%

Change since 1995 in spending for education .... +46%

Sources: U.S. Bureau of the Census & U.S. Bureau of Labor Statistics

and eyeglasses, but more on tickets to movies and sporting events, presumably for the whole family. One out of every three households in this age group has a pet and spends an average of $50 a month feeding and caring for it.

One expense that is likely to increase in the future (because of a decline in the perception of public-school quality) is tuition for private elementary and secondary schools. According to the Bureau of Labor Statistics, about 5 percent of all families headed by persons aged 35 to 44 send one or more of their kids to private school. In the process, they spend about $5,000 a year for tuition and other education-related items.

19 Older baby boomers are still a growing consumer market

For awesome buying power, it's hard to beat middle-aged baby boomers. The 21 million U.S. households headed by persons aged 45 to 54 have more aggregate income to spend than the entire economic output of Canada, our largest trading partner. And that already-large boomer income has been growing at nearly 10 percent per year since 1995.

By the end of this decade, 45-to-54-year-olds will be the largest ten-year age group in the United States. Between now and then, households in this age category will have increased another 12 to 14 percent to top out at around 24 million consumer units. Assuming that they continue to be the most affluent segment as well, these mature boomers might just be the strongest part of the consumer engine.

Because these older boomer households are such an important consumer market, we know a lot about them. Average household income peaks in this age bracket at over $73,000 a year, partly because more than one-fifth of households make $100,000 or more a year. More than three-quarters of householders aged 45 to 54 own their home and they have the most cars—2.4 vehicles per household, according to the Bureau of Labor Statistics.

One reason they have so many cars is that they have the most teenagers and the most kids in college. About one-half of the families in this age group have a child with a driver's license either at home or in college. For the average house-hold in this age bracket, education and transportation expenses combined eat up one-fifth of after-tax income.

Households in this age group also spend a lot on their home. This is often the age at which the home furnishings bought at least a decade ago begin to look a little dowdy. Since few of these families have any day-care expenses for young children, money can be spent on buying new home furnishings as well as exterior projects like gardens or landscaping.

Households aged 45 to 54 spend more than any other age group—over $40 billion a year—on home furnishings and equipment. A typical residential zip code with 5,000 homes would contain about 1,000 households in this age segment, and they could be expected to spend over $2 million a year on home furnishings.

Jewelry is big; apparel is not

Spending on apparel is no higher for this age group than for younger boomers, and spending for footwear is actually slightly lower. By age 50, keeping a fashionable wardrobe (or dressing up your older kids) does not appear to be a high priority. But spending on jewelry peaks in the 45-to-54 age group, at about 16 percent above that for younger households, so the market for watches, rings, and bracelets should remain strong.

By the time baby boomers are eligible to join the AARP, two categories of spending really take off—eyeglasses and medical services. Spending on medical services jumps 42 percent from ten years earlier, and spending on eyeglasses or

Older Boomers—Aged 45 to 54 (in 2000)

During the last half of the 1990s, the number of U.S. households with six-figure incomes ($100,000 or more) increased by 80 percent. By comparison, the total number of households edged up only 5 percent. One-third of all $100,000-plus income households are in the age range 45 to 54.

Average household income $73,100

Increase in average since 1995 .... +20%

Number of $100,000+ income households .... 4.2 million

Increase in such households since 1995 .... +77%

Change since 1995 in all household spending .... +16%

Change since 1995 in spending for health care .... +37%

Source: Bureau of the Census & Bureau of Labor Statistics

contact lenses increases 52 percent. Local providers of these services benefit, but it also suggests that all businesses need to be aware that as baby boomers age, they will spend more time and more money on health-related goods and services. Much of this spending is just to make them feel better.

What are you doing to make these customers feel better? Is the print big enough on your invoices or other reading material so no customer will have to squint? Many repair and service businesses have a place where customers can wait for service. How hard are the chairs and how long is the wait time before people become uncomfortable?

While older boomers spend much less than other households on athletic gear and beer, they spend the most of any age group on reading material—newspapers, magazines, and books. Households headed by persons aged 45 to 54 spend

32 percent more than average on all reading material and account for more than one out of every four dollars spent on books. It is an interesting fact that just as people's eyesight starts to deteriorate, they spend more time reading.

The spending statistics for this chapter all come from the large Consumer Expenditure Survey conducted annually by the U.S. Bureau of Labor Statistics. The primary purpose of the survey is to compute the Cost of Living Index that the bureau publishes, but this rich source of data on household spending for many demographic segments is available free at **http://www.bls.gov/csxhome.htm** for anyone who wishes to use it.

20 Watch for big changes among mature American consumers

When customers change, businesses must adapt or risk losing customers. But the problem is that most customer shifts happen over a decade or more and are slow enough that you might not notice them until a lot of sales are lost. This is particularly true when your customers get older or move and are replaced by people with different product or service preferences.

No better example of such customer shifting exists than the change happening among people in their late 50s and early 60s. The oldest baby boomer turned 55 in 2001. So over the next ten years, the segment aged 55 to 64 that was born before and during the Second World War will be completely replaced with boomers born in the more prosperous period after that war.

It is probably not just coincidence that General Motors made the decision in 2001 to stop producing the Oldsmobile, a popular car among people born before 1945, but a tough sell to those born later. Other products that are unable to adapt to changes in their older customers may meet the same fate, but not if incremental changes in marketing are designed to keep pace with the incremental changes in the marketplace.

Mature marketplace change

During the next decade, no ten-year age group in the U.S.

will change as much as the cohort aged 55 to 64. Now there are about 24 million people that age, but by 2010 there will be around 36 million—an increase of nearly 50 percent. By the end of this decade, about one in every six adults will be aged 55 to 64.

Overall U.S. population and household growth rates between now and 2010 are expected to average about 10 percent. By contrast, the number of households and married couples in this age segment will probably grow at about the same 50 percent rate, but the number of dual-earner households in the 55-to-64 age bracket will increase more than 100 percent.

The Bureau of Labor Statistics forecasts a 64 percent increase in the number of women aged 55 to 64 in the workforce, a growth rate more than four times that of all employed women.

That high growth in working women will be partly driven by the much higher levels of college education

---

Time of Change—Americans Aged 55 to 64

Changes in this age group's income and spending patterns over the next five years is expected to be far more extensive than over the past five years.

Median household income	$44,600
Increase in median 1995–2000	+17%
Number of $100,000+ income households	2.1 million
Increase in such households 1995–2000	+73%
Change in all household spending 1995–2000	+22%
Change in spending for wine 1995–2000	+68%

Sources: Bureau of the Census and Bureau of Labor Statistics

among women who were in high school during the late 1960s and 1970s. Many of these women are going to work to help put kids through college or to add to their own pension funds.

This vast change will likely result in a substantial increase in household income and spending power among households aged 55 to 64, which now have only a slightly above-average median income. In fact, the Census Bureau's latest income report shows a 15 percent drop in average household income for the group aged 45 to 54, which is ten years younger.

If that income drop disappears by 2010, which seems quite likely, it would mean an increase of over $200 billion in the aggregate spending power of households aged 55 to 64. What might they do with all that money? They could spend it, save it, or do some of each.

Spending changes and its beneficiaries

Given that baby boomers have not had a reputation as big savers, as they get closer to the usual retirement age, they may start saving or investing a bigger share of their income. But it is also likely that since they delayed marriage and children, they may have more college and other child-related expenses than the previous generation. It may also be that fewer of them will look at age 65 as the time when they will quit working.

There are several industries that are likely to benefit from high growth in both households and income among 55-to-64-year-olds, including financial services, housing, and travel. However, only the businesses in those sectors that anticipate the attitudes and product preferences of the boomers will benefit.

Whatever your industry, it's important to keep in mind this baby boomer mantra: "I want something unique!" For example, because of growing demand, the prices of some antiques have skyrocketed along with the popularity of the PBS show *Antiques Road Show.* And one of the more successful marketing magazines today, *1 to 1,* features stories about how to meet each customer's individual needs.

Among those aged 55 to 64, for example, nearly one in ten households own a vacation home, the most of any age group. This suggests that there may be a big jump in the demand for such homes. If so, there will likely be greater demand for architecturally unique homes than for cookie-cutter condominiums.

Since they delayed marriage and children, they may have more college and other child-related expenses than the previous generation.

Among 55-to-64-year-olds, the demand for wine also peaks for the more expensive special vintage wines, but not the sweet stuff with a screw top. Anyone in the full-service restaurant business that does not have a good wine list may miss this marketing opportunity completely.

There are literally hundreds of examples where baby boomers have abandoned previously popular products like Oldsmobile cars, much to the surprise of the suppliers. Changes in attitudes and product preferences over time should be expected for any market segment, but particularly so in this rapidly changing 55-to-64 age segment.

21 Senior households spend a lot on a few things

Retirement isn't what it used to be. Not many years ago, retirement at age 65 meant a big drop in family income and a drastic change in lifestyle. A generation ago, one in four people aged 65 and older lived in poverty. Today it's less than one in ten. Average household income for 65-to-74-year-olds now tops $40,000 a year—a 50 percent jump over ten years ago.

Among the reasons seniors are so much better off is that more people are choosing to work beyond age 65, and the value of their Individual Retirement Accounts or 401(k) plans has greatly increased, despite the market correction in 2001. During the past ten years, investment assets and dividend income for people aged 65 or older have more than doubled, while the average retired worker's Social Security check has increased by about 40 percent.

About 11.5 million

The number of households headed by someone aged 65 to 74 has remained fairly constant for the last decade. No change is expected in that number until later in this decade. By then we expect that one in four people aged 65 to 74 will be working or looking for work, up from one in five in the early 1990s. As a result, seniors' incomes are likely to grow even faster.

The Census Bureau reports that between 1995 and 1999, the number of households aged 65 to 74 with an annual income over $75,000 jumped by 49 percent. Given that rate of increase, there were at least 1.6 million senior households in that upper-income category in 2001. And as we would expect, rising income among these senior households has resulted in quite a bit more purchasing power.

Seniors spend more than you might think

Homeownership peaks in this age group, with 82 percent owning their home. Nearly three-quarters of home-owners aged 65 to 74 have no mortgage. Despite having no monthly mortgage payments, households in this age group still spend an average of about $30,000 a year, according to the Bureau of Labor Statistics. Excluding mortgage payments, that spending is close to the average for all U.S. households.

However, their spending patterns are anything but average. Since most senior households have only two people in them versus three for many younger households, we would expect them to spend less for the basics like food. They do, but not that much less. Senior households spend only 12 percent less than all households on food eaten at home. They spend about the same for fish, fruits, and vegetables, and they spend more than average on restaurant meals while traveling out of town.

Traveling is an important activity for households in this age group. They also are more likely than average to own a vacation home. Households aged 65 to 74 spend 24 percent more than all households on hotel or motel rooms and 47 percent more on vacation homes. Despite senior citizen discounts, they spend 27 percent more on airline fares and other means of travel and far more than any other age group renting recreational vehicles.

But less on some items

There are three categories where senior households spend a lot less than other households: clothing, cars, and entertainment. They spend 29 percent less on apparel and 25 percent less on buying, maintaining, and fueling their personal vehicles. When they do buy cars, they appear to have a decided preference for new over used.

Compared with the average household, senior households spend almost nothing on sound equipment or accessories, video games, or video rentals. But they spend the same as other households on cable TV. Generally, seniors spend less on admission to sports or other entertainment events. However, when they are traveling, they spend more.

Senior households spend 26 percent less than all households on furniture and floor coverings, but they spend 26 percent more on bath and bedroom linens, curtains and draperies. They spend about the same as other households on appliances, but much more for china, silverware, housekeeping services, and lawn or garden care.

Avid readers

Households aged 65 to 74 are periodical publishers' best customers. They spend the most of any age group on reading material—58 percent more on newspapers and 31 percent more on magazines. But they spend less on buying books, perhaps because they tend to visit a library more often than a bookstore.

The generous spirit of Americans is evident among senior households. They make cash contributions at a rate 42 percent higher than average, giving away over 6 percent of

Senior Households—Aged 65 to 74

Senior households spend far more for travel-related expenses than most households.

Median senior household income, 1999 .... $27,300

Increase in median 1995–2000 .... +19%

Number of $100,000+ senior households 760,000

Increase in such households 1995–2000 .... +46%

Change in all senior household spending 1995–2000 .... +18%

Source: Bureau of the Census and Bureau of Labor Statistics

their after-tax income—nearly $20 billion a year. Seniors also volunteer thousands of hours to community service organizations, helping to keep those non-profits viable.

It comes as no surprise that senior households spend more than the average household on health insurance (70 percent more), prescription drugs (104 percent), and related medical products such as eyeglasses and hearing aids (50 percent). Insurance helps with some medical expenses, however, and they spend less than average for all other medical care except dental.

Because the first baby boomer will turn 65 around 2010, the cohort aged 65 to 74 is expected to swell to 20 million households by 2020. During the next 10 to 20 years it will be interesting to watch how the spending and giving habits of this group change as the baby boom replaces the present members. Boomers will probably work longer and make more money. How they will spend it or give it away remains to be seen.

22 Elderly home-owner segment is growing rapidly

Better health care, rising life expectancy, and improved social networks have all contributed to making elderly households one of the fastest-growing household segments in America. One in every ten U.S. households is now headed by someone aged 75 or older, a 63 percent increase in the past 20 years, more than twice the growth rate of younger households.

Most elderly people live in their own homes. Three-quarters of the 10.4 million householders aged 75 or older are homeowners. Only about one in ten has a mortgage, but considering that the average elderly householder is 80 years old, it's surprising that only one-fourth choose to rent rather than own.

At this age, it may be more economical to own a home since so many get deep reductions on property taxes and few have mortgage payments. However, there are maintenance chores, and nearly half (46 percent) of the householders in this age group are elderly women who live alone. The Census Bureau doesn't count how many children of these homeowners spend part of their leisure time taking care of mom's house, but it must be in the millions.

Elderly householders fortunate enough to have investments have benefited greatly from asset appreciation and can probably pay somebody to mow the lawn. According to a Bureau of Labor Statistics survey, the value of their investments rose over 150 percent between 1995 and 2001. Their household income is rising as well, up 26 percent in the same period to an average of $28,000 a year. That may not sound like much, but there are over a million householders aged 75 or older whose household income exceeds $50,000 a year.

We expect that people aged 75 or older would be retired, but about 1 in 20 is employed or looking for work, a 40 percent increase over a decade ago, according to the Bureau of Labor Statistics. The bureau does not say what occupations they are in, but at age 80 we can be fairly sure they're not construction workers.

Some homeowners' costs can be high

Elderly households have an average of only 1.5 persons, the smallest of any age group. As we would expect, spending on basic items like food and clothing is way below average. Elderly households spend about one-half as much as other households on food, primarily because they spend so little on restaurant meals.

But many basic costs for homeownership are the same or higher than for other households. Elderly householders pay the same or slightly more for homeowner's insurance, maintenance and repair services, and security. And they pay about the same as others for most utilities, except for their low phone charges. They must either talk less or call collect.

Household operations, however, represent a greater share of expense for elderly homeowners. At this age, householders spend 36 percent of their after-tax income on all housing-related expenses. The average U.S. household spends only 30 percent for the same expenses. Elderly homeowners spend more than any other household age group on housekeeping services and more than twice as much as the average household for lawn and garden care.

They save in other areas, however. Householders aged 75 or older spend only half as much as other households on home furnishings and small appliances. The thrifty idea must be: if the old toaster works, why buy a new one? If that idea spreads, this economy is in real trouble.

Elderly households buy services rather than products

It seems like the older we get, the more we want or need things done for us rather than doing them ourselves. So the growth in the number of elderly households has created a huge service industry that will do everything from asset management to zipping around to do errands.

A lot of spending by households in the 75-or-older category is for some kind of household or personal service—an

---

Elderly Households Aged 75 or Older Becoming More Comfortable

Elderly households contribute over $8 billion to non-profit organizations.

Median elderly household income	$20,000
Increase in median 1995 to 2000	+25%
Number of $100,000+ income elderly households	330,000
Increase in such households 1995 to 2000	+122%
Change 1995-2000 in all elderly household spending	+22%
Increase 1995-2000 in cash contributions	+56%

Source: Bureau of the Census and Bureau of Labor Statistics

aggregate of at least $70 billion. And there is growing demand for household services such as cleaning, repairs, or home maintenance, as well as for personal services such as medical or health maintenance services, meal delivery, financial services, or transportation services.

Compared with the elderly of a generation ago, many more of today's seniors live in their own homes. As the population aged 75 or older continues to grow, living longer and by themselves, the service industry that takes care of them and their homes can only get larger.

23 Married-couple trends are important to businesses

Married couples are the heart and soul of consumer spending in America. They spend more in a week on their kids, homes, and cars than many other families spend in a month. So keeping up on marriage and family trends is vital for anyone who provides consumer goods or services.

There are now about 55 million married-couple families in the U.S., according to the Census Bureau, and they are only a bare majority (52 percent) of all households. Twenty years ago, there were about 50 million married couples, and they were three-fifths of all households. So they have grown much more slowly than other types of households, edging up only 13 percent over the past two decades, versus a 35

Household Size Continues to Shrink

Household and family size continues to decline but at a slower rate than past decades.

AVERAGE NUMBER OF PERSONS:	2000	1990	CHANGE
In all households	2.59	2.63	- 1.5%
In all families	3.14	3.16	- 0.6%

Source: Census Bureau

percent increase in non-families and a 60 percent jump in other families, which include single parents.

The number of married couples with children, now at about 25 million, has not changed significantly in 30 years. Fewer than one of every four households in the U.S. (24 percent) is a married couple with children. Married couples with two or more children are 15 percent of households— only one in every seven. So much for mom, pop, and two kids as "typical."

Relatively small but big in buying power

While their numbers are not growing much, married-couple family income, which averages more than $70,000, is the highest of any household type and growing rapidly. Married couples with children have an average income that's even higher. It varies from about $70,000 a year for those with younger children to nearly $80,000 for those with older children. Married couples now dominate the six-figure-income category.

While married couples are only a bare majority of households, they are over 80 percent of all households with an income that exceeds $100,000 a year and 77 percent of all households earning between $75,000 and $100,000 a year. And half of those affluent families have children under age 18.

One of the reasons that there are so many high-income married couples is the phenomenon of people in similar professional occupations marrying each other. In the past, it was unusual for two doctors or two attorneys to marry each other, because there were so few women in those professions. Now it is quite common, and both spouses usually

Married Couples' Household Income

In three-quarters of married couples where the husband works, the wife is also employed full- or part-time.

WORK CATEGORY	NUMBER IN 2001	AVERAGE INCOME, 2000
All married couples	55.6 million	$74,100
Husband works	44.5	83,100
Wife works	33.5	87,000
Both work FTYR*	18.0	94,000

* FTYR= full-time year-round

Source: Census Bureau

keep working. The effect is to combine two high incomes into one very affluent household.

But whatever their occupations, most married-couple households have two earners, particularly if they have children. More than six in ten married women with preschool children are either employed or looking for work, despite the high cost of child care. Once the children go to school, more than three-quarters of their moms go off to work.

Anyone who has ever experienced having a job while caring for a family knows how stressful that can be and how little time is available for things like shopping. Since the vast majority of married couples with children have internet connections, any supplier of goods and services to this market would certainly benefit from having a web site and a delivery service that make shopping more convenient for these big spenders.

According to the Bureau of Labor Statistics, married couples account for two-thirds of all consumer spending.

Married with Kids—Hardly the Majority Today

Married couples are a bare majority, and those with children are only one in four households. Parents with preschoolers are less than one in six households.

	NUMBER IN 2000	PERCENT OF TOTAL
All U.S. households	104.7 million	100%
All families	72.0	69
Married couples	55.3	53
with children	26.4	25
Other families	16.7	16
with children	10.9	10
Non-families	32.7	31

Source: Census Bureau

But in some categories, it's an even bigger share. For example, married-couple households buy three-quarters of all photographic equipment, sports equipment, recreational gear, and life insurance.

Married-couple myths

One myth about married couples is that it is not a stable lifestyle choice because half of all marriages end in divorce. This myth persists because each year over the past decade, there has been roughly one divorce for every two marriages. However, dividing one of those numbers into the other makes no sense without taking into account the base from which they occur.

Each year, there are about 1.2 million divorces from a pool of over 50 million married couples. So in an average year, only about 2 percent of all existing marriages end in divorce. In that same year, there are about 2.4 million marriages, about half of which are remarriages.

The bottom line is that more than 95 percent of Americans get married at some point, and according to a Census Bureau survey, at most only about one-third of the respondents report ever having been divorced. While it is true that more couples are choosing to live together without being married, it appears that the institution of marriage is still vital.

Growth in highly educated consumers

Among the most interesting consumer segments are those with high educational attainment. The Census Bureau reports that between 1995 and 2000 the number of households headed by people with advanced degrees (master's, professional or doctorate) has increased 11 percent, twice the rate of growth for all households.

Nationwide, about one in every ten households has such high educational attainment. But the census will show that there is wide variation from place to place. Communities with a college, a university, or corporate headquarters almost always have more people with advanced degrees, while retirement communities generally have fewer.

The concentration in any one place may be less important today since the vast majority of this market segment have internet access either at home or at work. From a customer service point of view, what this means is that they are likely to be extremely well-informed consumers who

Percent Change 1995 to 2000*

The number of highly educated women is increasing faster than that of their male counterparts, and their median income is rising more rapidly as well, up 34 percent since 1995 versus a 26 percent increase for men.

	PERCENT CHANGE 1995 TO 2000*
Men	+11%
Women	+23%

*In persons aged 25+ with advanced degrees

Source: Census Bureau

want more printed or web-based information about what they are buying.

Highly educated consumers are also more likely to purchase custom-made or locally made household goods, such as pottery, rather than mass-produced branded items. According to Mediamark Research, households in this market segment are heavy consumers of printed matter such as books, magazines, and newspapers, but are less likely to watch network television.

Considering that this consumer group is growing at twice the rate of all households, has a median income that often exceeds $100,000, and spends heavily on personal services and locally made goods, this is a market segment worth watching.

24 Find out what your customers want to know

In the benchmark year 2000, the oldest baby boomers were 54 years old and the youngest would have been 36. In just a couple of years, the largest age group of consumers—one in five adults—will be people in their 40s. We're talking about some high earners here as well as major-league consumers.

People in their 40s are also nearly all employed. According to the Bureau of Labor Statistics, 88 percent of men and 75 percent of women in that age group are working. And never before have so many worked in white-collar jobs. About half the men and three-quarters of employed women work in managerial, professional, or other office-based occupations.

What this means is that more of your customers than ever before have some business or professional experience and are better informed customers as a result. They are more likely to have access to the internet and can comparison shop without leaving their homes or offices. They are far more likely to search for some information about what they intend to buy before going shopping.

So ordinary consumer goods that have no unique qualities are probably going to be bought at the place with the lowest prices. But since a small business can almost never be profitable competing on price, how can you be competitive?

There are several ways to prosper in what may appear to be a brutally price-driven marketplace. One way is to com-

Highly Paid Workers

The number of highly paid women workers has more than doubled in the past five years.

	YRFT * WORKERS	CHANGE 1995–2000	EARNING $75,000+	CHANGE 1995–2000
Men	58.8 million	+11.6%	9.5 million	+88.1%
Women	41.6 million	+17.2%	2.2 million	+145.6%

*Year-round full-time workers
Source: Census Bureau March 2001 Survey

pletely differentiate what you provide by creating a unique buying experience, creating one-of-a-kind goods, or offering an extraordinary level of service and product knowledge that exceeds what your customers normally expect.

Furniture is a good example. With new homes built larger than ever before and more people than ever before in their peak earning years, the demand for furniture should be rising. But so much furniture looks and feels similar that price becomes dominant. What may be lacking on the part of customers is an understanding of how to evaluate quality, service, and interior design.

The furniture business, like many other businesses, could benefit from a big infusion of information for more-savvy customers. Furniture customers usually visit a showroom and see items displayed in a number of settings. But suppose they could also sit at a large screen console showing selected pieces of upholstered furniture with complete information about who made it, how it was made, and its quality attributes.

Twenty-First Century Workers

The 2000 census found that women are now nearly half of all employed persons. But they are a clear majority of professional, office and administrative workers.

OCCUPATION	MEN	WOMEN
2000 census counts	69.8 million	60.4 million
Managers and finance workers	14.9%	12.4%
Professional workers	16.3	23.3
Sales workers	10.7	11.8
Office and administrative workers	7.3	24.9
Service workers	12.3	18.4
Construction workers	10.2	0.4
Production workers	10.6	5.9
Transport workers	9.8	2.2
Other workers	7.9	0.7
Total	100.0%	100.0%

Source: Census Bureau

The same screen could also show the piece in a range of fabric choices with a background of various matching draperies or other coordinating items—essentially creating a virtual room. The sales person then becomes a facilitator who helps customers create unique interior environments for their homes. Perhaps then price will no longer be the determining factor in the sale.

How much is too much?

Every business is different in some way, but almost all businesses would benefit from the marketing concept that consumers want to be better-informed customers—but only somewhat better informed. There is such a thing as too much information.

There are audiophiles, for example, who want to know the detailed technical specs on every piece of sound equipment they buy. But most of us tin-eared consumers just want something that sounds okay and doesn't look too outlandish or complicated. We also want to have the way things work explained in simple but not condescending terms.

There is a marketing advantage to be gained by gauging just how much information customers want and what kind. The more you offer, the more likely it is that customers will come to believe that they can get the full story from you and not just marketing hype.

So think about ways you could better inform customers that will increase their confidence in you and make them more likely to return. Remember, information is an important service that more customers will value highly.

25 Anxiety may influence what homeowners buy

During the 1950s many homeowners, fearful of nuclear war, built bomb shelters in their backyards and stocked them with canned food and bottles of water. During this decade, we may see a variation on that theme. Because of the increased sense of vulnerability in large cities, we may now see a significant increase in the purchase of small second homes in rural areas where people might flee in the event of another attack.

The powerful emotion of fear may add to the other factors that are already at work to boost the ownership of second homes some distance from major metropolitan areas. What may happen is that people who were already thinking about buying a vacation residence will do it sooner than they might have in more normal times.

The rational reason for buying another home is to use it occasionally for vacations or on weekends. For that purpose, only about one in twenty U.S. households owns a second home. But mortgage rates are now quite attractive, and in most cases the interest on both home mortgages is tax deductible.

In addition to the financial and emotional reasons, there is a powerful demographic driver pushing this phenomenon. Second homes are most often bought by households in the 55-to-64-year-old market cluster, a consumer segment that is increasing at four to five times the rate of all households.

Seasonal, Recreational, and Occasional-Use Homes in U.S.

During the 1990s, more than 50,000 second homes were built each year.

NUMBER	PERCENT OF OWNER-OCCUPIED UNITS	CHANGE 1990 TO 2000
3.6 million	5.1%	+16.1%

Source: Census 2000

Households in that age group are nearly twice as likely as other households to purchase a second residence.

A big increase in the purchase and use of second homes has important implications for local businesses, because it means that people are not at their primary residence as often as they would be if they owned only one home. And the second home is most often more than a hundred miles from the community where people normally reside and shop.

The census taken in April 2000 counted people and households at their primary residence. The census questionnaire did not ask where you were on weekends or holidays or at the height of summer or the low of winter. But the census is the base from which most estimates of consumer market potential are made.

This suggests that in the future, businesses wishing to estimate market potential or market growth may need to conduct some customer research of their own. The market area you serve, for example, may contain customers who occasionally visit their second home in your market area, as well as customers who are occasionally elsewhere.

The growth of the second-home phenomenon means seasonal swings in business activity may be even wider than they are now. Developing a marketing strategy that attempts to broaden your customer base may help to even out cash flow. Many retailers, such as garden suppliers, are already familiar with seasonal swings and adjust their operations accordingly.

But a deeper understanding of where customers are at different times of the week or year may reveal new business opportunities. For example, if you find out that more of your customers are out of town on weekends, perhaps longer evening hours one or two days during the week or an e-commerce-equipped web site might be beneficial.

Since average homeowners spend between one-quarter and one-third of their income on their primary residence, being away from it periodically may alter their home-based spending. For example, people with two homes may be more likely to buy maintenance services or security systems than those who usually stay home on weekends.

It is likely that the waves of fear so many people feel will gradually fade and consumer behavior will become somewhat more predictable. But that may take years, so in the meantime, it's important to learn more about what your customers are doing with their time and how they may be changing their lifestyles.

If more of them are spending their weekends or holidays or even a whole season away from your community, perhaps the only way to find out is to ask them. But whether they have one home or two, there has never been a time where conversing with your customers either by survey or in person has been more central to the future of your business.

Part IV

Building strong customer relationships

26 Put more focus on high-interest customers

A fun part of any business is talking to customers who are really interested in what you're selling. The hard part is trying to sell something to those folks who just don't care. It's a lot like teaching, where the most fun is in helping those kids who really want to learn.

The way to put more fun in your business is to develop what I call a "best customer strategy," the objective of which is to focus more attention on the high-interest customers and pay less attention to the low-involvement ones.

A major benefit of this strategy is that it will almost certainly make your business grow because high-interest customers are usually the ones who spend the most money. Another benefit is that more interested customers can lift employee morale. This is particularly important because the biggest problem for many businesses today is finding and keeping good employees.

Developing a best customer strategy is not time consuming, but it is never ending. In the day-to-day stress of operating a business, it is all too easy to let your best customer strategy slide. The trick to making it work is to set aside just a little time each week or even each month to focus on who your customers are and how to attract more of the best ones.

Three-part process

Step one is an information-gathering process involving all your customers. The objective is to learn how high-interest customers are different from others. The idea is to record the differences in their purchasing behavior and find out how their demographic profile or other characteristics are unique.

Suppose, for example, that you have a business selling indoor plants and flowers. You can survey your customers to find out something about them, but it's much easier to check first with your trade association or the government agency that surveys consumers.

According to the Bureau of Labor Statistics (BLS) annual consumer surveys (www.bls.gov/csxhome.htm), only about one in five (20 percent) households buy indoor plants or fresh flowers. The BLS reports that the average American household spends about $54 a year on such purchases, but households aged 45 to 64 spend between $74 and $84 a year.

The BLS further reports that households with high income ($70,000 or more) or high educational attainment are more likely to buy plants and flowers (one in three) and spend more than twice as much as average—over $115 a year. These facts are from a nationwide survey, so it's a good idea to periodically confirm that your best customers have similar characteristics. Then it's time to go on to step two.

Step two is to find out where there might be concentrations of people with the above demographic characteristics. The 2000 census will be helpful in that regard. In addition to the geographic location, it is important to identify the media preferences of your best customers. Any advertising sales person should be able to tell you what part of his readers, listeners, or viewers have the characteristics of your best customers. Then you can choose where to advertise to reach the best prospects most efficiently.

A poorly worded ad will always deliver disappointing results, and the temptation will be to blame the media.

It is not enough, however, to find the most efficient media buy. What you say in your advertisements is equally, if not more, important. A poorly worded ad will always deliver disappointing results, and the temptation will be to blame the media. Better to take the time to prepare an advertisement that is worded to directly appeal to the demographic target you have identified as likely to become best customers. That's what step three is all about.

Step three is to create a simple system for regularly conversing with your best customers. It can be done via e-mail, by telephone, or even in person. However it is done, the purpose is to systematically discover what they most like about doing business with you. That may be your main competitive advantage, which could form the basis for your next ad campaign.

While communicating with your customers, you may also find out what other goods or services they would like you to provide. This is important because lack of knowledge about what customers really want can cause huge opportunity loss and stunt your business growth. My experience has been that conversations with my customers provided many more ideas for successful new products or services than any ideas I thought up without customer involvement.

By conversing regularly with your customers you might discover that they really like your personal guarantee of high-quality plants. (Another advertising theme?) Or you could find that they would like you to provide more booklets on the proper care and feeding of their plants. A more in-depth conversation might suggest that a houseplant-care service for people on vacation could be a new source of revenue.

Developing a best customer strategy that includes research to find out more about who they are and regular structured conversations to find out more about what they really want can be fun as well as profitable. It may even help you develop more effective advertising themes, the subject of another chapter.

27 Brand equity can be your most valuable asset

A brand name can become the most valuable thing your company owns. Other business assets such as inventory or equipment may become worthless or obsolete by changing technology. But a well-recognized brand name is a piece of intellectual property that can increase customer loyalty in the short term but also retain substantial value long term.

The reason a brand name is worth so much and has such lasting value is that it exists in the minds of customers or potential customers, not in a warehouse or company office. Once the image of a brand, and what it stands for, is firmly implanted in customers' minds, it can create instant positive recall and generate business for many decades.

Creating a brand name with lasting value, however, is not so easily done. A brand is an intangible thing, the value of which is sometimes difficult to measure or justify funding. It's a lot easier to buy things you can see and account for like a bigger sign or more promotional materials. Investing in building your brand name, however, does not always involve spending money. Investments in brand development can pay huge dividends in future years. Here's how.

Maintain the focus

Think about all the major brand names that you can instantly recall: names like Ford, IBM, or Kodak. As soon as you think of their name, you can immediately say what they do or what they make. If Ford were to start marketing toasters instead of cars and trucks, you would think they had lost their minds, and you'd be right.

But many smaller firms with far more limited resources often try to do several things or try several different marketing themes in an effort to find one that seems to bring in the most business. Inevitably, the result is just a lot of confused customers who have no clear idea what the business is or what benefit it offers them.

Successful brand building starts with a total focus on the customer's wants or needs and the single most important benefit for those customers. Is it top-quality merchandise? Is it superior service with a satisfaction guarantee? Is it a promise of zero defects? Or is it just a lifetime warranty?

The point is this: how well customers remember your brand name will depend on how well you deliver on a benefit that they (not you!) think is important.

Make a brand promise

A brand becomes truly valuable when it is instantly connected in many customers' minds with a promise of one thing that those customers value highly. So perhaps the most important step in building brand value is to make a brand promise, which often takes the form of a tag line, a slogan, or a short written pledge to customers.

Writing down a good brand promise is easier to do than it is to actually fulfill that promise. Once you promise that the service is guaranteed or the product is flawless, you had better come through. Few things can ruin a business faster than bitterly disappointed customers. So before making any promises to customers, be sure your business has in place the personnel and systems it needs to profitably deliver what you have told those customers to expect.

Once you design your business to deliver the benefit you have promised, however, you will get paid back at least twice. The first thing you get is a competitive advantage because your brand name will be remembered more often. Second, your customers will nearly always pay more for the benefits you promise. Consumers have long shown a willingness to pay more for a branded product than an unbranded one.

Consistently support your brand

Brand value is built and maintained by consistently delivering on your brand promise and by consistent advertising. The volume and frequency of your advertising should, of course, be appropriate to the size and nature of your business. But the central benefit message should always be prominent and immediately recognizable.

After a few years, customers should be able to identify your firm by your ads even if your name is obscured. This is important because quite often people see or hear only a fragment of an advertisement for a second or two. If your marketing messages have been consistent, those fragments should still work for you and generate business.

Probably the most important thing any firm can do to build its brand's value is to resist the urge to change its basic marketing message or the look and feel of its advertising. If sales start trending down, for example, it's easy to think that the marketing message is at fault, when in fact, it could be many other things.

During an economic slowdown, firms often cut back on advertising. When sales fall off, many may think that what they need is a different ad campaign. In most cases, what is called for is a little market research to find out what's really going on.

Building brand value requires a total commitment to focus all marketing efforts on the one most important benefit that your product or service delivers. Maintaining such focus and clarity of purpose over a long period of time is not easy. But over time, the additional value you have created will become very evident in loyal repeat customers and increased value of your business.

28 Capture customers, forget fame

Fame often has no payoff. Just because a big part of your region's population knows your name may not make any of them change their buying habits. Nearly everyone can remember one or two now extinct dot-com companies, or at least their clever TV ads. But their celebrity status didn't bring them any sustainable business.

In the bricks-and-mortar world, many small locally owned stores have closed as customers migrated to national retailers and big shopping centers. Years after those small stores are gone, local folks remember many of them fondly. But that awareness and even fondness didn't translate into enough sales to keep them in business.

So what does it take to motivate customers to start spending more money with you and not somewhere else? It takes an awareness of what prospective customers really need as opposed to what you may think they need. And it means looking at your entire marketing plan to be sure it's building your business and not just making you locally famous.

Focus on customers' real problems

When you see customers or talk to them on the telephone, they probably have things on their minds that have nothing to do with what you are selling. They may be worried about losing their jobs or stressed out about something else, which may mean they are mentally preparing to have a problem in this buying encounter.

This suggests the marketing practice of frequently meeting with employees who are in contact with customers to get feedback on what customers are saying or how they are acting. It also means thinking about ways to have thoughtful dialogue with customers and coming up with creative ways to exceed customers' expectations for service.

Be sure the customer goes away with the feeling that you understood the problem and did your best to help.

For example, a customer may ask for an item or service you don't provide. However, your employees can be instructed to give the customer as much help as possible. Can the item be special ordered? Is there another place of business nearby that might have the item? Can you call the store and find out, thus saving the customer another fruitless trip if it is not available? If the customer is on the telephone, can you supply the telephone number of another possible source? The objective should be to make sure the customer goes away with the feeling that you understood the problem and did your best to help.

Even if a business couldn't help you, think how much more likely you would be to return if you were given the kind of assistance described above. You might also provide the added incentive of giving the customer a coupon that could be applied to a future visit.

Focus your advertising on your best value proposition

Attracting valuable repeat customers should be the objective of your advertising. If it also builds awareness, that's nice, but your advertising's effectiveness should be measured on its sales impact. For maximum impact, each ad should have some copy or a tagline that clearly states your best value proposition.

What is your best value proposition? Is it best quality, best service, widest possible choices, lowest prices, or something else? The idea is to use advertising, promotional activities, and any other interactions with prospects to put your establishment at the very top of their minds when they begin thinking about the things you provide.

Take, for example, a not-yet-well-known college that has a fabulous language program and several ways that its students can study abroad for a semester or two. It also has a continuing-education program and a great network of alumni to assist graduates throughout their careers.

The college's best value proposition is that it does an outstanding job of preparing students to work in organizations that are increasingly worldwide in scope. And it stays in touch after you graduate. How could it state its best value proposition on all its marketing materials? Here's one idea: "A global education for life."

Focus on your niche and forget the rest

Most small businesses, and even some pretty large ones, appeal to a very small segment of the population. That segment may be geographically small or demographically tiny. But either way, it pays to get to know your niche really well.

And it pays to have your niche know you very well too. If your business is providing childcare, clothing, or anything else for children, for example, your marketing may be wasted on most households. Only about one-third of households have any children, and even if we count grandparents, we have a hard time getting up to 50 percent.

But in some neighborhoods (particularly Hispanic ones), the vast majority of households have kids. The 2000 census details where those neighborhoods are and how many families are in them. You should be really well known in those areas and target market to those households with children, and maybe a couple of grandparents as well. The rest of the households need only be dimly aware of who you are.

The bottom line is, if you want to be famous, become a performer. If you want to be more successful at your business, focus your energy on understanding your customers' needs, creating a meaningful value proposition for them, and figuring out how to best serve them.

29 Employees are critical to marketing success

When two of us are being chased by a wild bear, I don't have to run faster than the bear. I just need to be in front of you by a second or two. That gruesome truth illustrates a key principle of business survival. It's not necessary to get everything perfect. But it is necessary to be at least a step or two ahead of competitors who are already out there.

In today's highly competitive consumer and business marketplace, success may happen because you have a somewhat better product or service, but not necessarily. That's because most consumers have neither the time nor the knowledge to discern most differences in quality. More often, it is the superior marketing that makes the difference in profitability and survival, because that's what customers can see and it's what they will act on.

Achieving superior marketing, however, means a lot more than just having a catchy slogan or clever advertisements. It means improving more of the mundane details involved in customer interactions to the point where potential customers always think of you first, even if only by a second or two. Here are a few of those details.

Involve your employees

This is the most often neglected part of marketing because it is so hard. Human resource management is, in my view, the most difficult part of running any business. It is time consuming, often frustrated by human frailties, and never ending. But the most successful businesses in America are the ones that make employees proud to say where they work and motivated to do their best for the customers.

The best marketing begins with a staff meeting. The worst marketing comes as a surprise to employees. How often have you called a firm in response to an ad only to get a befuddled response from an obviously uninformed employee? Much of the ad campaign expenses were probably wasted right there.

By contrast, starting a new marketing campaign by talking with employees has the advantages of bringing out their creativity and their knowledge of customer needs. And any employee re-
sponses to customer inquiries will then match your marketing messages. Testing advertising themes on employees can also avoid any credibility gap between what you say to potential customers and what you can actually deliver.

Workers who take care of happy customers get great enjoyment out of their work.

But the most important reason for involving employees at the planning stage of any marketing effort is because it sends the clear message that you understand how important they are to the success of your enterprise and that you value their input. If you don't value your employees' comments, you probably need to rethink your hiring process.

Build better customer relationships, not just sales

Some important research has been done recently that quantifies the huge advantage a firm gets by working to retain customers rather than just marketing to get new ones.

The latest term being used to describe this strategy is customer relationship management, or CRM. It should be called CS for common sense because it must be pretty obvious that if you take good care of your best customers, they will keep coming back and save you the big expense of constantly looking for new ones.

That bit of common sense turns out to be seldom practiced because it means using all short-term profits for the not-so-glamorous work of careful recruitment and extensive training of employees and the tedious work of detailed market research. Only a small percentage of entrepreneurs have that kind of patience.

But those who do also benefit from having high employee morale and low turnover because workers who take care of happy customers get great enjoyment out of their work—another breakthrough piece of common sense. A good book that shows just how profitable this can be is *The Service Profit Chain* published by The Free Press.

Keep pace with your customer base

Customers change. They get older and their needs change. They often move away and new people with new wants and needs move in. The 2000 census tells us what every other census has told us: America is a constantly changing mosaic of people. Firms that do not keep pace with changing consumer markets risk seeing their customers just disappear.

Now that census data are here, it's a good time to find out how the community you serve has changed in the past decade. If it's growing, where is the growth coming from? Across the nation, nearly half (40 percent) of all growth was

Customer Loyalty Pays Off

Profit increase from just a 5 percent increase in customer loyalty.

BUSINESS TYPE	PROFIT INCREASE
Auto service	30%
Industrial goods	45
Office management	40
Software	35
Branch banks	85
Credit cards	75
Credit insurance	25
Insurance brokerage	50
Industrial laundry	45
Average 9 business types	48

Source: The Service Profit Chain *published by* The Free Press

due to the increase in the Hispanic population. Since the Hispanic population is much younger than average, in areas of high Hispanic growth, we can expect growing demand for youth-oriented products and services.

But many communities have fewer residents than they did in 1990 due to out-migration, fewer births, or both. Since it is usually young people who move, a community that is not growing is aging more rapidly than average. That will almost certainly cause shifts in consumer demand away from youth-oriented products and services.

30 Customers define quality

Both large and small fortunes have been lost by business people who were absolutely certain they knew what customers wanted. The biggest losses in recent years have come from the now defunct dot-com retailers who bet billions on the premise that millions wanted to buy everything online and that all the customers cared about was low price.

But every day, somewhat smaller fortunes are lost by storefront retailers or restaurant owners who forget that, in addition to good-quality merchandise or food, people also expect prompt service and a clean place. During the busy days of starting or running any business, it's easy to forget that customers arrive online or offline with a concept of quality in their minds that is probably not what you think it is.

There are, of course, a few business owners who seem to have an instinct for offering exactly what customers want. But like singers with perfect pitch, they are the exception rather than the rule. Most of us do not have perfect pitch, and it's best if we don't bet the ranch on our ability to predict what combination of price and quality customers will want most.

We have all had personal experiences with going shopping, dining out, or buying some kind of service, and the sum of those experiences can create the impression that we know what high quality is. That may be true, but chances are that our personal opinions do not do a very good job at predicting consumer behavior.

Take restaurant meals, for example. Some are served on fine china, while others are served on paper or plastic plates. You may think that only good china is acceptable. But restaurant customers in general are far more likely to define high quality by how the food tastes and the overall experience than by how the plate looks.

Unlike in countries where home computers and good telephone service are not common, cyber cafes have not been very successful in the U.S. because people come into a restaurant expecting to have a meal and perhaps some conversation with their companions. The presence of computers only detracts from the quality of the dining experience, as do cellular telephones.

Customer expectations evolve

One of the more difficult marketing challenges that all businesses face is that customers' expectations of quality changes. Just think about how much better quality we have come to expect of our cars, computers, home appliances, and many other products. What was a quite acceptable car ten years ago, for example, would be a tough sell to today's drivers.

It's the same regarding customer service. Perhaps it's the influence of the internet, but customers now seem to have much less patience. Whether it's waiting for the phone to be answered, standing in line, or expecting to get something delivered, the amount of time that people will wait before getting irritated seems to be getting shorter every year.

From a marketing point of view, the fact that customers' concept of quality evolves can be turned into a distinct competitive advantage. This is because many businesses that have been around awhile often develop a comfortable selling groove. They offer basically the same products or level of service they did last year or the year before without really paying attention to how their customers' attitudes about quality are changing.

The reason is that those customer attitudes probably don't change at all from month to month. But in the day-to-day management of a business, operational costs and other things can change quickly and require immediate attention. To get a marketing advantage, it's really just a matter of marking a calendar and every quarter or every six months soliciting customer feedback, listening to it, and adjusting operations accordingly.

Customer expectations can be compared to yours

By asking customers to rate various aspects of your business, you can quickly discover what's important to them versus what's important to you. For example, two things that are costly and often important to small-magazine publishers, winning a National Magazine Award and printing on top-quality paper, are rarely noticed by subscribers or advertisers.

Perhaps there is some aspect of your business that's expensive and important to you, but your customers either do not notice or do not care. It may be personally difficult, but ultimately necessary for business survival, to shift those resources to improve the quality of the things that customers do care about so they do not go elsewhere.

The bottom line is that, every day, business managers must make decisions about what to spend money on to improve quality and what to say about quality in advertising to prospective customers. Knowing what customers think is important will make those decisions easier as well as make whatever is spent on marketing a lot more productive.

31 Develop the unique benefits of your business

Every eight seconds during an average American business day, someone starts another business. To survive, each of those businesses needs some kind of a competitive edge. That edge can take many forms, but the most sustainable long-term advantage comes from developing, maintaining, and promoting a unique selling proposition.

Think about the businesses that you visit or call frequently. What is it that keeps you coming back? Is it friendly staff or superior service? Perhaps the products they sell are of better variety and quality or maybe they deliver faster? Is it just that you think their prices are lower or is it that their business hours are more convenient for you? Maybe it's some combination of the above factors that converted you to a regular customer.

Whatever the reasons, they are probably no accident. Someone at those businesses thought about what it was going to take to rise above the average and attract more frequent customers. Deciding what one feature or benefit of your business is unique is important because great marketing advantage accrues to the "best" or the "first" or the "top" business in any category.

Be different

Developing your unique selling proposition is a matter of finding out what it is about your business that is most ben-

---

New Business Start-Ups by Industry

Most new businesses deliver some kind of service or engage in retail or wholesale trade. Fewer than one in ten businesses are incorporated to manufacture a product. Over the past 5 years (1994 to 1999), the number of new business starts has declined 20 percent, but the number of workers hired by those businesses has increased by 22 percent, suggesting that each new business is, on average, hiring more workers.

INDUSTRY	PERCENT OF TOTAL
Business and personal services	34%
Retail and wholesale trade	30
Construction	11
Financial services	9
Manufacturing	8
Transportation and utilities	6
Agriculture and mining	2
Total	100%

Source: Dun & Bradstreet

---

eficial to the customer and can't be easily duplicated. Having somewhat longer business hours might be beneficial, for example, but others could easily stay open as long or longer.

Being different often means finding an unmet need. Consider the case of the experienced dog groomer who wanted to open her own shop but saw a crowded field in her area, where more than two dozen establishments specialized in grooming pets. However, a little research uncovered a gap. None of the existing providers made house calls. The prevalence of more elderly pet owners as well as households with two fully employed adults suggested the need for the service.

So she bought a specially equipped van and started with this unique selling proposition: we pick up your pets, clean them up, exercise them while you are at work, and even take them to the vet for shots and check-ups. Her web site and van had a picture of a running horse with dogs and cats alongside to help customers remember the name of the business: Greta's Galloping Groomer.

Be memorable

Your marketing advantage comes from the fact that your unique selling proposition will be the one thing potential customers will remember about your business and your advertising. Most people are not very good at remembering numbers or an unconnected business name, so it is unlikely that after seeing even several of your marketing messages, they will remember any pricing information or your name.

On the other hand, if you can convey in just a few words a compelling benefit of visiting your business, they will remember that, and your advertising will be a lot more effective. The point of any advertising or promotional activity is to cut through the vast amount of information and advertising that consumers view in a day and get them to think of your business when the need for what you sell arises—days, weeks or even months later.

One way to do that is to try to use a word or two from your unique selling proposition in the name of your business. If that is not possible, the next best thing is a short memorable tagline, which should always appear wherever the name of the business appears—not just in advertisements.

The best tagline is a brand promise such as, "We Guarantee your pet will feel better." Part of a unique selling proposition is to convey the promise that your business delivers something extraordinary and guarantees it as well.

Be relevant

To be memorable and bring in customers, a unique selling proposition needs to be credible, sustainable, and relevant. Making a claim to be the "best computer service" is too broad and subjective and not likely to be believed. Saying that you have "top technical expertise" might be more credible. But is it sustainable? Such a claim might only work until another business starts advertising that it has more experts on its staff.

But the real question about any advertising claim is this: is it relevant to the customers' needs? Frequently, competitors start throwing around claims of superiority about something that doesn't matter much to customers. For example, at one time, personal-computer makers competed on the basis of speed and RAM when what customers wanted was a more reliable machine that didn't crash so often.

After seeing many thousands of commercials making all manner of claims, consumers have become suspicious of marketing slogans with no substance behind them. So if you are going to develop a unique selling proposition, it can't be just an advertising tagline or an empty promise. If it is, the loss of credibility will stifle any repeat business.

A unique selling proposition should really be at the heart of why a business exists. It should reflect the desires of the owners and employees to provide something that has unique benefits for customers and will sustain the business for many years. The bottom line is that the most successful and long-lived unique selling propositions are not the ones quickly done for an ad campaign, but the ones that are in harmony with the reasons why the business was created.

32 Invest in expertise for your employees, or lose them

Knowledgeable employees are the key to any successful marketing program. Not having enough well-informed employees to provide superior customer service can greatly diminish the benefit of an otherwise effective advertising or promotion campaign.

Retaining skilled workers has always been important, but in the coming years, it is going to take on a sense of urgency as the gap between the demand for employees and the number of people looking for work widens. This seems hard to believe when it seems like there are so many unemployed people looking for work.

But that will change. According to a new report by the Bureau of Labor Statistics, labor force growth during this decade will not match the number of new job openings that need to be filled. This is good news for those just graduating from school, but bad news for employers who have no desire to revisit the tight labor markets of the late 1990s.

Bureau economists predict that for every 100 job openings during this decade, there may be as few as 76 people looking for work. And even that dire forecast assumes a significant increase in women joining the workforce. That may occur, but some recent data showed a slight decline in labor force participation of women who have small children.

Projected Job Growth by Industry

Business services are one of the nation's fastest-growing industries.

INDUSTRY	CHANGE 2000 TO 2008
Manufacturing	+ 1%
Retail trade	+ 10
Finance	+ 10
Services	+ 22
Health care	+ 25
Business services	+ 34
All industry average	+11

Source: Bureau of Labor Statistics

The thing to keep in mind about these forecasts is that they are for the nation as a whole, and the situation can be much better or much worse in specific locations. For example, in a state like New York, which has had a high out-migration of workers in the past, labor shortages may be worse. But in states like California and New Hampshire, heavy in-migration may soften the effects of the nation-wide trend.

The aging workforce

Not only is the labor force failing to serve up enough workers, but it's getting older too. By the end of this decade, the bureau predicts that, on average, the workforce will be older than it has ever been since they started keeping statistics. They see a workforce in 2010 in which more than one-half of the workers will be over age 40.

21ˢᵗ Century Workforce

The fastest growth will be among more experienced workers aged 45 or older.

AGE GROUP	PERCENT OF TOTAL (2000)	PERCENT CHANGE 2000 TO 2010
Under 25	16.1%	+15%
25 to 34	22.5	+8
35 to 44	26.9	-10
45 to 54	21.6	+21
55 to 64	9.9	+52
65 or older	3.0	+30
Total workforce	100.0%	+12

Source: Bureau of Labor Statistics

Labor department economists also predict that as more previously non-working people go to work, 67.5 percent of people aged 16 and older will be either at work or looking for work, a 30-year record. The bureau also foresees a workforce that will be nearly half (48 percent) women.

From a marketing point of view, this is great news, because people with jobs buy more goods and services than people without jobs. However, for that to continue, there must be enough workers to make those goods and deliver those services.

There are only a couple of ways to increase the size of the workforce in the short term. One way is to allow more immigration. But the terrorist attacks of September 11, 2001, make that less likely. Another way is to pay enough to lure people out of retirement. That might work. The bureau predicts that an additional 1.2 million people aged 65 or older will join the workforce between now and 2010.

A third way is to increase the productivity of workers so that you don't need so many of them. In the old sweatshop days, that just meant making people work longer hours, and there has been some of that in recent years. But the better way is to increase the skills of workers and thus make them more productive in the longer term.

According to bureau economists, most new jobs will require only work-related training, but the most rapidly growing jobs require some education beyond high school. Whatever is needed, the bottom line is that the best investment employers can make today is to increase the expertise of their employees. Better-educated workers will be more productive as well as better informed, and as a result, they will provide superior customer service.

When labor shortages return, the employer with the better-trained customer service staff will have a distinct competitive advantage. That advantage will probably translate into higher compensation for the employees, which usually means less turnover.

Finally, here are a few of the fastest-growing occupations between now and 2010 that you could suggest to young people. Suggest nursing (1 million job openings) or other health-care occupations (another 3.6 million job openings), or becoming a primary or secondary school teacher (1.6 million job openings). If they like working with food, bureau forecasters predict a need for 6.3 million cooks, food-preparation workers, and other related workers.

33 How to think about the future of your enterprise

During traumatic and uncertain times, it is difficult to think about the future. But if you don't plan for the future of your enterprise, then uncertainty and fear may cloud whatever you might want to accomplish. Customers, employees, and others depend on business enterprises to provide leadership and some vision of what their future might be despite the uncertainties.

At times like these, many firms return to the fundamentals and think about the value of what they provide and the relationships they have with their customers. If those relationships are strong and the value proposition substantial, then planning for next year is a matter of deciding how best to serve your customers given the present circumstances.

The fundamental questions to ask when planning for the future of your business enterprise are still the same: How are customers' needs changing? What will they expect from us? How can we provide them products and services more efficiently? Finding answers to these questions can help managers make decisions about how to conduct business in the future.

Customers' needs change all the time

Any set of customers will alter their buying behavior if one or more of these three things change: their economic situation, their demographic characteristics, or their attitudes. People who lose their jobs, for example, will almost certainly postpone or forego many purchases, but when people get married, have children, and get older, their changed demographic circumstances mean a more permanent shift in consumer behavior.

An attitudinal shift, however, can also change consumer behavior. Just reading about a decline in the index of consumer confidence or about how many other people have lost their jobs can be unsettling and influence a customer's decision at the point of purchase.

It is important when making future plans to distinguish between temporary changes in economic circumstances or consumer sentiment and more long-lasting demographic changes or fundamental attitudinal shifts. Short-term shifts may alter buying behavior for a few months or quarters, but they can also mask long-term basic changes in consumer behavior that last for decades.

During times of economic stress, businesses frequently postpone development of new products or services and stick with what they have provided for years. That might be a prudent strategy for a few months, but it may also cause sales to decline longer term.

If what your customers want or need is changing in some fundamental way, you need to adapt to those changes rather than assume things will return to their previous state in a few months.

If, for example, your customers are people in their 20s, their product preferences will probably change quite dramatically over the next ten years. If your customers are primarily older families with teenage kids, their purchase be-

Changing Consumer Households

The two fastest-growing household types are also among the smallest; each is less than one in every ten households. Married couples are still the majority of all households.

HOUSEHOLD TYPE	NUMBER (MILLIONS)	CHANGE 1990-2000
Married couples with children	24.8 million	+ 6%
Married couples without children	29.7	+9
Single parents	9.8	+32
Other families	7.5	+2
People who live alone	27.2	+21
Other non-family households	6.5	+33
All households	105.5	+15

Source: U.S. Census Bureau

havior will probably change a lot when they become empty nesters.

In the past, it might have been possible to wait for the next crop of customers to come along. However, sharp declines in the size of age groups, such as what is happening now in the 35-to-44 age group, makes that a problematic and possibly expensive strategy. In addition, product preferences often change from one generation to the next, and you need to anticipate those changes.

A more successful marketing strategy might be to stay in close touch with your customers, survey them frequently, and find out how you might be able to alter your products and services, or create new ones, to serve them better as their needs change. The new data from the 2000 census may also reveal how customers in your shopping area have changed during the past decade and how they are likely to change in the future.

One of the things to look for is a long-term change in what consumers value. In the short run, consumers may not buy certain goods or services because they are fearful and think they shouldn't spend money at the moment. But a permanent change in what consumers value has contributed to some consumers avoiding tobacco products, hard liquor, and to some extent red meat. Money doesn't make the difference. A change in values does.

When forecasting sales, the basics are the same regardless of the economic circumstances. It's a matter of estimating how many potential customers are in your market area and then making a determination of how much each one of them is going to spend on what you offer. The part that requires some work is forecasting how the number of potential customers might change and then determining if their purchasing behavior will also change.

Difficult times make it hard to focus on the fundamentals. But the businesses that recover the best from those times will be the ones that maintain good customer relationships and adapt to long-term changes in consumer preferences.

34 Your customers may have a new outlook

Some customer attributes, such as age, change little from month to month. But your customers' minds and attitudes can change overnight and have a profound effect on their consumer behavior. In 2001, the immense tragedy of the September 11th attack was a life-changing event for many Americans, and it may alter what they do with their lives and lifestyles for years to come.

We are now in uncharted marketing territory, because nothing like this has happened before. In the past, when explorers went into unfamiliar terrain, they usually proceeded cautiously because they were afraid of what might happen. We are now in a situation where many consumers and businesses are, quite understandably, proceeding with great caution even though in most places the familiar patterns of life seem to be returning.

One effect the catastrophe may have is to reduce the appeal of things that are outrageous or superficial and increase the desirability of long-term personal and business relationships. Building good customer relationships has always been a key part of any marketing plan, but now it's essential to get that right.

This is probably a time when putting your customers at ease and not on edge is critical. Simple and straightforward marketing messages that err on the side of a soft sell are likely to be more effective than a hard sell. Paying attention to how customers are feeling, making them comfortable, and avoiding confrontation has never been more important.

One of the central elements of brand marketing is that buying a known brand, or buying from somebody a customer knows, lowers the chance of buying an inferior product or getting bad service. In marketing your brand or your firm today, emphasizing the guaranteed quality aspect of what you sell is likely to resonate with consumers who probably don't feel like taking any chances.

There are few places where Americans feel safer and more in control than in their cars.

When buying frequently purchased and relatively inexpensive goods, most consumers look for the lowest price and assume a certain level of risk with regard to quality. But if more of our purchases are services and consumers become more risk averse, businesses may need to focus more of their marketing efforts on building and maintaining genuine customer relationships.

If more people are fearful of what might happen next, we may see an increase in the desire to just stay home. If people spend more time at home, they may be inclined to fix the place up or buy more furnishings or decorative items for their home. Rather than going shopping they may also want more goods delivered.

In a time of heightened fear of crowded places or large buildings, people may also want to be able to work at home if they need to, thus increasing the demand for high-speed internet connections and other communications gear necessary for a home office.

In times of high stress, there is also a greater desire to somehow regain a sense of personal control over some aspect of one's life. This often manifests itself by people driving more when they do leave home. There are few places where Americans feel safer and more in control than in their cars. It's an illusion, of course, but the result may be even more traffic and less use of public transportation than we have now.

Sooner or later, Americans will start traveling again for recreational purposes, and when they do, it is likely that more of them will go by car. This suggests that hotels, restaurants, and other businesses that cater to tourists would be well advised to try some marketing in communities that are about a day's drive away. In times of uncertainty, vacationers may want to stay fairly close to home.

It surely comes as no surprise to any business person to

U.S. Population—Big-City Dwellers versus Country Folk

More than one-quarter of U.S. residents live in cities of 100,000 people or more. One in every 35 U.S. residents lives in New York, the nation's largest city. More people live in the nation's 9 largest cities than all of the 1,580 smallest counties.

RESIDENTS OF	PEOPLE	SHARE OF U.S. POPULATION	PERCENT CHANGE 1990–2000
New York City	8.0 million	3%	+9.4%
9 cities of 1 million+	22.9	8	+10.0
243 cities of 100,000+	76.1	27	+11.4
1,580 counties with fewer than 25,000	18.7	7	+8.3
U.S. total	281.4	100	+13.2

Source: Census Bureau, 2000 census

hear that consumers do not always act rationally. There has probably never been a safer time to fly, but Americans are avoiding airports in huge numbers. It is likely that the public will someday get over its fear of flying, but if so, nobody knows when.

It is also likely that someday U.S. consumer markets will return to normal, whatever that is, but no one is quite sure when. In the meantime, the best advice seems to be: act like an early explorer and proceed cautiously.

35 Nobel Prize confirms it: more customer knowledge equals more profits

The 2001 Nobel Prize in Economics went to three American economists for their research into the idea that economic transactions are less efficient (translation: somebody makes less money) when buyers or sellers have unequal access to key information.

Here's another way to say that: When you haven't a clue as to what customers value, or even who they are, it becomes much harder to find the right prices that will meet your profit goals. The equally important other side of that prize-winning research is that if the customers know little about the quality of what they are buying from you, they will pay less.

What a simple concept. Educated customers are your best customers because they are more likely to know the value of what they are buying. And marketing with information about customers is more efficient than marketing without it.

But what the economists left for the marketing folks to figure out was how to get better informed about customers and how to get better-informed customers. Such is always the gap between prize-winning theoretical research and the practical application of that research, where the only prize you get is enough profit to stay in business.

Making better-informed customers

If customers are uninformed, it may be because your marketing is not very informative. Advertisements that only talk about price most likely do not convey enough information about value. For example, is a $20 bottle of wine twice as good as a $10 bottle? Anyone who buys wine learns pretty quickly that there may be no difference at all or that the $10 bottle actually tastes better.

Perhaps the people selling the $10 bottle would benefit from having some customer research that told them what simple words occasional wine drinkers (and not the so-called experts) used to describe a great tasting bottle of wine. Then they could use those words in advertisements or packaging and perhaps get $12 or $13 instead of $10.

But look at it from a new customer's point of view. Why should they take a chance on the more expensive bottle, only to find that it tastes terrible? Why not put an 800 number or a web-site address on the bottle encouraging customers to call or write and tell you how it tasted to them? If a customer complains about wasting 20 bucks on your product, you then have a golden opportunity to offer a meaningful coupon on one of your other products that may be more to the customer's liking.

Now wine, like other alcoholic beverages, is heavily regulated by state liquor laws. So couponing is undoubtedly forbidden somewhere, which probably makes it impossible everywhere. But getting customers to call or write you with comments is certainly legal and the knowledge gained from the conversation, not to mention the possible database of customer addresses, can be used to create and target more effective advertising.

Wine Buyers Are Hardly Average Consumers

Households reporting that they bought wine, by income level:

	ALL CONSUMER UNITS	INCOME $50,000-$75,000	INCOME $75,000+
BOUGHT WINE:			
At home	7%	8%	14%
At full-service restaurants	11%	14%	22%
SPENDING INDEX:			
Food at home	100	124	144
Dinner at full-service restaurants	100	122	227

Source: Bureau of Labor Statistics

Making better-informed marketing decisions

Wine that comes in a bottle with a cork is most often consumed with food eaten at home or in a full-service restaurant. In either case, the person buying wine is likely to spend more on the food than the person who doesn't buy any wine. How do we know this?

We know this because the Bureau of Labor Statistics asks a representative sample of about 7,500 households if they buy wine and how much they spend on it as well as how much they spend for food to be consumed at home and how much they spend for dinner at full-service restaurants.

Suppose that you own a food store or a full-service restaurant. Householders who are the most likely to buy wine spend 1.44 times the average household on food at home and more than twice as much (2.27 times more) on dinners at full-service restaurants. These wine drinkers probably represent only about one in every four customers, but a far larger share of total revenue and profits.

If there were ever a customer group that should be surveyed about customer satisfaction issues, this is it. Keeping just a few of these folks coming back can be worth many times the cost of a small post-card survey put into the shopping bag or given with the check.

In your next survey, you don't have to ask the intrusive and seldom-answered question about income. Just ask them a couple of questions about wine.

But if you are in some other business, how is this relevant to you? Well, it turns out that households who are most likely to buy wine and spend the most on it also have an income of $75,000 a year or more. So in your next survey, you don't have to ask the intrusive and seldom-answered question about income. Just ask them a couple of questions about wine.

Such high-income households also spend a lot more on many, but not all, consumer products and services. So identifying them may be very helpful when crafting your next marketing campaign, if they are an important market segment for your business.

A Nobel Prize winner also gets a check for $1 million. But the application of the concept that captured the prize for this year's winners in economics can be worth much more than that to any business person who wants to make use of it.

36 Privacy should be of concern to all

Privacy is an evolving concept and a customer service mine field. Businesses need to learn more about their customers in order to serve them better. But collecting that information today means treading carefully between learning about important customer attributes such as age or home address and stepping on what customers consider private ground.

Most people understand that they will have to provide private and personal financial information in order to get a bank loan. But they often resent having to provide their home address just to buy something simple, like an appliance or a bottle of wine. That resentment happens because of heightened fears that somehow in the record of their purchase activity their privacy will be compromised.

Prior to the widespread use of computerized databases, Americans didn't think much about privacy, because the details of their every transaction, or every transgression, were not recorded for viewing by any firm that bought access to those details. But they are now, and one result is an increasingly well-founded belief that every piece of information you reveal may be used at best for telemarketing purposes or at worst to deny you insurance.

Enough horror stories about the abuse of consumer data have been reported that few buyers believe that any company will keep their personal information confidential. And that's a problem for the thousands of honest business people who want to create customer databases in order to develop products that more closely match what people want and to deliver better customer service.

Part of the difficulty is that the concept of what is private varies greatly from person to person and from product to product. If, for example, the person who changes the oil in your car or cleans your teeth (hopefully not the same person) wants your home address to remind you of your next appointment, very few people would be concerned that somehow that information would be sold and their privacy violated.

Customers respond well to customized offers. They do not respond well to the improper use of their personal information.

That's because, like most mundane business transactions, nobody cares, except the buyer and the one small business involved. Not so with other more sensitive purchases, such as prescription drugs, alcoholic beverages, tobacco products, or reading material. In those cases, privacy can be a very big deal indeed, because information about some of those purchases, if revealed, can be used in extremely harmful ways.

Respect all privacy concerns

Since there is a rising fear about loss of privacy, the sensible way to proceed is to assume the customer is always concerned about it and allay their fears by having a clearly stated privacy policy on your web site as well as printed for any customer to pick up. Another way is to make providing addresses or other personal information as optional as you can, and tell the customer why you are asking for it, and how you intend to use it.

Breaching customer confidentiality is the third rail of customer relations. So don't even go near it, because once people lose trust in you to keep what you learn about them to yourself, they will avoid your business. The simplest way to avoid this problem is to use common sense and only obtain marketing information that is essential to your operations.

The age question

One useful bit of knowledge for marketing purposes, for example, is the customer's age. Many businesses segment their customers by age and tailor marketing messages to age groups that they know are more likely to respond. Nothing wrong with that, unless one of your customers gets something from you that says: "Now that you've turned 50, come in for our special offer…" Chances are, you just lost a customer forever.

No matter what you may learn about a customer, reminding them that you know their age, income, or size of their home is always a mistake. Savvy customers know that frequently an offer is being made to them because a business has some information that suggests a higher-than-average probability of making a sale. That's the essence of target marketing, which is often done with an effectiveness that results in lower marketing costs, and ultimately, in lower prices.

But being effective does not mean being explicit about what that information is. Just make the offer and track what happens. Customers respond well to customized offers. They do not respond well to the improper use of their personal information. Successful marketing sometimes means using personal data to create special offers, but always while being sensitive to your customers' need for personal privacy.

37 Preserving customer loyalty

Customer loyalty is the most precious, but intangible, company asset. That's because loyalty is a concept that exists only in the customer's mind. Unlike buildings or equipment, loyalty is hard to quantify and impossible to buy or make quickly. But it can be more important to business success than anything on the balance sheet.

Customers return to a business many times because of a set of factors—any one of which can go off track without any obvious sign that something is wrong. Nobody rings a bell when the perceived quality of a product or service starts to decline or when the demand for what you provide starts dropping because of changing wants or needs.

A few customers may say something, but most often they just stop coming. And it probably does not have anything to do with external factors like the slowing economy, which is the usual suspect. That's why regular dialogue with customers is such an important component in building and maintaining customer loyalty.

There are many ways to converse with customers, but a systematic program of asking for customer feedback has many benefits. Periodically asking customers a few questions can provide a benchmark as well as a moving picture of how customers rate your product or service. But it can also show how their needs or expectations might be changing.

Separate the best from the worst

Perhaps the most overlooked aspect of regularly asking for customers' opinions, however, is that it can alert you to a new kind of customer segmentation. You can find out which segment is most happy with what you provide, which ones are reasonably satisfied, and which ones are almost never satisfied no matter what you do. Finding out which customers to say goodbye to can do wonders for your bottom line, not to mention the enamel on your teeth.

Nobody rings a bell when the perceived quality of a product or service starts to decline.

Let there be no doubt. Your most profitable customers will be those who are most satisfied with what you provide and who come back over and over again. By contrast, the ones who are almost never satisfied are rarely profitable either.

Once you determine which segment is the happiest with what you provide, the next task is to determine what elements contribute to their high level of satisfaction and repeat purchase behavior. Perhaps it is the friendly and knowledgeable staff, or the consistently high quality, or the competitive prices, or something else. The important thing is to find out what it is so you can be sure to stay on top of that aspect of your business.

Asking questions always beats assuming

Possibly the biggest mistake in marketing is to assume that you know what keeps customers coming back. You might get lucky once or twice, but more often than not you'll be surprised. For example, you might think it's low prices that keep customers returning, but what really brings them back is the wide selection of things you have in stock.

One way to get customers' opinions about what they like and don't like is to ask them in a survey. This can be done immediately following their purchase of the product or service, or on a schedule that makes sense for your business. For example, a restaurant or hotel should provide the survey right after the meal or the stay. But a concert hall or theatre might send patrons a survey at the end of the season.

The main purpose of such a survey is to establish the level of customer satisfaction and to gauge the level of customer loyalty. So perhaps the first question should be along this line: "How satisfied were you with the service you received from us?" The choice of answers can range from "completely satisfied" to "extremely dissatisfied," with follow-up questions for any dissatisfied answer.

Homeowners with Mortgages

People aged 55 to 64 live in the most expensive homes, but those over age 64 have the fewest mortgages.

AGE OF HOMEOWNER	PERCENT WITH MORTGAGE	HOME VALUE INDEX (100=AVER.)
25 to 34	82%	60
35 to 44	80	108
45 to 54	72	124
55 to 64	51	142
65 or older	22	110
Average	60	100

Source: Bureau of Labor Statistics

The loyalty question goes something like this: "How likely are you to call on us next time you purchase ...?" The respondent is given a choice in how to answer, for example: "definitely will," "probably will," "maybe," "probably will not," or "definitely will not." Those who answer that they will probably or definitely not return must then be offered an opportunity to tell you why.

Comments from satisfied and loyal customers may be some of the most valuable advertising copy you could buy.

If at all possible, try to get an address or phone number from all respondents so you can, if you wish, send back something to thank the loyal customers and win back a momentarily dissatisfied one. But in any case, over a period of time, the results of asking customers for their opinions regarding your operation will provide valuable information about customers' likes and dislikes and what things they value the most.

A big bonus from asking questions is that comments from satisfied and loyal customers may be some of the most valuable advertising copy you could buy, while comments from customers who are not returning may be just the management tool you need to fix those things that drive otherwise happy customers away.

38 Remember: there are no free lunches

Anyone with business experience knows this truth: There are no free lunches. The freedoms, rights, and protections we enjoy come with a number of obligations and no guarantees of success. One of those obligations is to deal fairly and honestly with customers, employees, shareholders, and other stakeholders in your business.

Those obligations are important because free markets work to the benefit of the most people in an atmosphere of trust. Customers, for example, have a right to expect accuracy and truthfulness from your marketing messages, within the normal bounds of hyperbole in advertising copy.

Straightforwardness in marketing is a great asset as well as a winning long-term strategy. Lack of truthfulness can make a short-term sale or advantageous business deal, but customers and former partners can have very long memories of being cheated or getting poor-quality goods, and they will probably tell others about it as well.

Obtaining a quick sale at the cost of customer trust is not a recipe for business longevity. Patience and honesty may be virtues, but they are a necessity for staying in business long term. There is simply no getting around the fact that it takes a long time to establish a good brand name and solid customer relationships.

In the frenzy of internet start-ups, some entrepreneurs suggested that the rules had changed and that long-term customers and market share could be bought quickly with venture capital billions. They found out, in a very expensive way, that freedom from failure is not among the rights we enjoy.

Every community has businesses that have been there seemingly forever. What is often lost in its history is how long it took to establish that business. Any entrepreneur who is still in business can tell you about how they gave up short-term profits for longer-term gain.

Those same entrepreneurs can also tell you about how difficult it is to become profitable when critical information about their marketplace is murky or nonexistent. One of the reasons that so many start-ups in the U.S. make it is the vast amount of business statistics gathered and published by various federal agencies.

Many of the same business people who complain about not having enough information to make good business decisions are the ones who won't return their questionnaires.

But those numbers, which are nearly always readily available on the web, are not free. The Census Bureau and other federal statistical agencies depend on businesses and individuals to complete questionnaires and return them promptly. Yet many of the same business people who complain about not having enough information to make good business decisions are the ones who won't return their questionnaires, citing privacy concerns.

Yes, we all make mistakes, particularly those of us who have started businesses. The trick is to be able to distinguish between fatal and non-fatal mistakes and to do everything possible to avoid making the fatal ones. Making that distinction is a lot easier if you are guided by certain principles.

One way to assess the wisdom of making a business deal is to ask how you would feel if your family and friends read about it in tomorrow's paper. If you cringe at the thought, perhaps it's not such a good idea after all.

Reading about it in tomorrow's paper is a great example of transparency—everything is visible and nothing is "under the table." Customers value transparency highly because it gives them a feeling of confidence that they are dealing with a business that is going to treat them fairly and honestly.

The advantages of good business practices multiply because customers will keep coming back and will often pay a premium for being treated well. It bears repeating: there are no free lunches. Being straightforward with your marketing messages and business dealings may mean some lost sales, but in the long run, it's both the best marketing tactic as well as the most winning business strategy.

Part V

Marketing, selling, and advertising

39 Now is the time to plant some seeds of knowledge

Each business reacts differently to a business slowdown. Some lay off as many people as they can and just try to survive until better times. But others use down time to gather knowledge and make plans to revitalize their business so they will be ready when customers are in a better mood to spend money.

When business is booming, there may be no time and maybe no need to sharpen your marketing skills. But when business slows, there is no better time to seek out and put in place some fresh marketing ideas. Those who overcome the tendency to do nothing will reap the benefits of learning about changing customer wants and needs as well as more effective ways to fulfill them.

There are at least a couple of ways to increase your marketing knowledge. One way is to attend a seminar given by the American Marketing Association (AMA). A lower-budget way is to read one or two of the better books on marketing. So here is a review of one AMA seminar and one marketing book publisher, both of which can offer you some useful marketing knowledge.

Marketing Seminars

The American Marketing Association offers a basic day and a half marketing seminar a couple of times a month in a variety of locations. It costs between $400 and $600 depending on whether or not you are a member of the AMA. To find the next one nearest to you go to **www.marketingpower .com** (type bootcamp in the search box), or call **800-262-1150.**

Despite its unfortunate name "Marketing Boot Camp," the seminars provide an excellent review of the basics along with some fresh concepts. Nobody made the attendees march around the room when I attended, but the seminar leader interacted with the audience in a very customer-friendly way that was a good marketing lesson all by itself.

The other important marketing lessons delivered with examples and case studies were these:

First, find what singular benefit you offer and convert it into a sustainable competitive advantage.

Second, constantly gather and use information about your customers and your industry to reevaluate your business and your marketing strategy.

Third, create targeted marketing messages aimed at the consumer segment you serve that promote the attributes of your product or service that are most valued by those customers.

The seminar was a reminder of how important a good marketing plan is to an organization's success and how many unforeseen problems can occur when there is no plan. Writing a plan often seems impossible because a vital part of any marketing plan is the honest assessment of your strengths and weaknesses as well as a realistic estimate of your business opportunities and roadblocks to your success.

Self assessment is always difficult, and one of the benefits of interactive training programs is learning what you can do versus what you should get someone else to do. We don't do our own oral surgery, and there may be some aspects of a marketing plan we shouldn't do either.

Good books

For those whose learning style tilts toward reading, there are a few books on marketing that may be helpful. In general, read anything by Peter Drucker. His ideas are without peer. Also some of the classic, but perhaps out-of-print books by Al Ries and Jack Trout such as *Marketing Warfare* and *Positioning: The Battle for Your Mind,* still provide valuable insights years after they were published.

Two other writers offer both practical tips and useful marketing ideas in their very readable books. Both *Sales Promotion Essentials,* by Don E. Schultz, and *Strategic Database Marketing,* by Arthur M. Hughes, are inexpensive and available from Paramount Market Publishing. Their web site is: **www.paramountbooks.com** or call them at **888-787-8100** for a free catalog.

Whether you choose the seminar route or the book route to enhance your marketing knowledge, the increased awareness of how to be more successful with your enterprise will serve you well.

Plan your way out of uncertainty

It's hard to imagine a time of greater uncertainty. The impact of the unprecedented attacks on our country and disruptions of war combined with recession-driven job losses have made many consumers and businesses understandably very concerned about future prospects.

The multiple levels of uncertainty make planning for the

future more difficult, but it is also more important than ever because planning provides a much needed sense of control. If the last year or two have been ordinary ones, then next year's plan could be guided by the past. But sometimes, the plan for next year must begin with a clean sheet of paper and a list of questions.

Asking questions such as: "When are things going to get back to normal?" are not helpful because there are no useful answers. On the other hand, trying to find answers to questions about your customers is always helpful. For example: "How are the people in the area we serve changing and how might they behave differently next year?" The answer to that question could help you feel a lot better about what next year might bring.

We don't do our own oral surgery, and there may be some aspects of a marketing plan we shouldn't do either.

Some people suggest that planning in chaotic times is a waste of time, because no one knows what will happen next. Well, future events are nearly always unknown. But you can be reasonably certain of this: if your marketing is more effective, more customers will appear. Planning to improve your marketing effectiveness is probably one of the most profitable ways you can spend your time.

The most valuable marketing plans start with a focus on past customers and possible future customers. Plans that start with a pared down ad budget put the cart before the horse. Gaining more knowledge about customers and how best to reach them leads to an appropriate advertising budget, not the other way around.

Suppose, for example, that you have determined what

geographic area your customers come from and how that area is defined by neighborhoods, towns, cities or zip codes. Census data (www.census.gov) can tell you how many people live in that area as well as their demographic characteristics.

That information provides the number of potential customers and whether or not the area is growing. A comparison of the demographic data from the 1990 census with the 2000 census reveals how the area may have changed over the past decade. Chances are that people in your trading area are now older and somewhat more affluent, even if they don't seem to be in much of a mood to spend their money right now.

It's always a good idea to check with your local county or municipal planning office to verify the trends you identify using census data. Things could have changed in the past few years that may not be fully described by a once-a-decade census. But in most cases, census data can go a long way to answering the question: "How are my customers changing?"

What the census can never tell you is how your customers might behave differently next year. This is because the Census Bureau does not ask Americans how they feel, even though it might make for some really interesting census data. Attitudinal questions are left to the private pollsters and survey research firms.

But one does not need to be an expert survey researcher to determine that people are becoming more cautious. Considering the enormity of events in September 2001, it would be a miracle if Americans were not more cautious and risk averse in the years ahead.

A heightened aversion to risk means that consumers may

be more likely to stick with places and products they know and trust. This suggests that advertising themes reminding your customers how long you have been a part of their community are likely to resonate particularly well. Any guarantees of quality or performance that you can provide will serve you well by reducing any element of risk your customers might feel.

Planning to improve your marketing effectiveness is one of the most profitable ways you can spend your time.

The best way to find out how you customers are feeling, however, is to ask them either formally through a survey or informally through conversations. The objective of learning about consumer attitudes is to understand how to communicate more effectively with your customers and prospects in the future.

When working on your marketing plan for next year, keep in mind that it is the combination of and the interaction between changing demographics and shifting attitudes that mainly drive consumer behavior. If one of your objectives is to make your marketing efforts work better than they have in the past, then focus your planning process on those two attributes of your customers and see what a difference it can make.

40 Marketing and selling are not interchangeable

To most people, the words marketing and selling are interchangeable. That's too bad, because in this information age, marketing is less about hard selling and more about using knowledge to more closely match what you offer to the needs of customers.

When you are there with the right service or product at or near the time when a potential customer needs it or is thinking about buying it, there is a lot less selling involved. Finding out how many potential customers are in the area where you conduct business and measuring the extent of their wants or needs is the essence of information-based marketing.

The benefits of consumer surveys

When you don't know what customers need, selling is hard work and is more often unrewarding. Information-based marketing is a lot easier, but it involves two things that most people are afraid of—risk and statistics.

You risk finding out that there is insufficient need for what you are selling, and you need to find a new way to make a living. However, risk is an inherent part of any business.

Statistics are always scary in the abstract, but the stats on what people buy are readily available, and when you get up close to them, they can seem reasonably friendly. There is, for example, an information resource that provides two of the essential elements needed for information-based marketing: demographics and purchasing behavior.

That resource is an annual survey program that queries a large random sample of U.S. households about all their purchases. It's actually two surveys, appropriately called the Consumer Expenditure Surveys. They are conducted by the Bureau of the Census for the Bureau of Labor Statistics. The central purpose of these two surveys is to create benchmark data for adjusting the Consumer Price Index, but the spin-off benefit is the creation of a comprehensive source of spending data for information-based marketing.

One of the surveys is a quarterly interview of 7,500 households. In this survey, the interviewers collect information about everything for which the households have spent money during the prior three months. They also collect data on the age, income, and other demographics of those households. The other survey asks another 7,500 households to record in a diary everything (no matter how small) that they purchased or gave away over two consecutive one-week periods.

The resulting tables of data (because of strict confidentiality rules, there is no information on individuals) provide a useful picture of how much money different demographic segments spent on goods and services. All that is necessary for you to make optimal use of this resource is to know which demographic segment most of your customers come from.

Suppose, for example, that you have observed that most of your customers appear to be well educated. College-educated consumers represent only a little more than one in four households. But according to the weekly diaries described above, more than half of those college graduate households reported going out to dinner that week. They also reported spending nearly 50 percent more than other households on fish and seafood to eat at home.

If you are in the restaurant business, you can connect the dots and sell additional meals by offering more fish or seafood on the menu. It's the same for many other consumer goods and services. The combination of knowing the demographics of your customers and finding out how much, on average, they are spending can make selling to them a lot easier.

Uncover new opportunities

The Consumer Expenditure Survey is even more useful for spotting new business opportunities. Suppose, for example

Five-Year Spending Trends

Spending on educational services is growing at more than twice the average rate.

CATEGORY	CHANGE 1994 TO 1999
Food at home	+ 8%
Food away from home	+25
Apparel	+ 6
Educational services	+38
Cash contributions	+23
All spending average	+17

Source: Bureau of Labor Statistics

that you have seen the 2000 census data for your community, and it confirmed what you have personally observed: an increase of people with graying hair. Now the census does not ask hair color, of course, but it does ask age, and it reported increasing numbers of 45-to-64-year-olds—when most hair needs color.

Most people might shrug off those facts as further proof that we are all not as young as we used to be. But if you're interested in finding a new marketing opportunity, the combination of high growth among the older age segments and spending trends from the Consumer Expenditure Surveys can point to growing demand for certain goods and services.

The reason is that those surveys are conducted annually and the data are easily obtainable from 1990 to 2000 as well as other years on the Bureau of Labor Statistics website. The site is **www.bls.gov/cxshome.htm**. Since the BLS reports on hundreds of categories of consumer goods and services, you can almost certainly find something to help you understand how best to serve your customers and make the job of selling to them easier.

41 Good marketing ideas all pass the common-sense test

What's the difference between a good marketing idea and one that sounds good, but is far more costly? They both claim to increase sales and profits, but one fails the common sense test. Among the many good customer-focused marketing ideas, very few require expensive software and services. But remember that there are pricey business marketing fads similar to those in fashion apparel.

The latest "new concept" in marketing always seems to require a three-letter acronym, which of course is designed to create the illusion of complexity, and justify the high price. A few years ago it was DBM, which was shorthand for database marketing. That describes a very straightforward idea: put what information you know about your customers in a computer database and use it to market to them more efficiently. Pretty simple, eh?

Database marketing, or DBM, must have been too simple, because it's now been replaced with vastly more expensive CRM or Customer Relationship Management. After all the hype about "optimizing complex knowledge-based relationship solutions," what CRM does is—you guessed it—database marketing.

The widespread belief that customer relationships need to be "managed" is an admission that too many businesses have forgotten why they exist. Customer relationships are what every business and marketing manager should be thinking about every day. If the interaction between a business and its customers is faltering, it is unlikely that just some new CRM software is going to make it better.

The most classic example of this is what has happened to 800-number customer service. You spend an incredibly long time on hold, finally to be greeted by a pleasant customer representative who has all the CRM software to see what's going on with your account. But does all that technology solve your problem with the firm's products or services? Rarely.

Lessons from this "solution"

What can be learned from this latest marketing fad? First, that it's easier to implement a technical solution that promises to fix everything than it is to ask the hard questions about why customers are not returning. If customers are not happy, perhaps it's a personnel or quality problem rather than a marketing problem that needs to be fixed.

Second, having a customer relationship, like having any relationship, means dialogue, not one-way sales talk driven by software. There is simply no substitute for conversing with customers, surveying customers, or otherwise soliciting their comments. It doesn't mean that you have to implement every suggestion that customers make. But people will feel better about your firm if they think you are really listening to them and improving operations as a result.

Third, customer relationships are not something that needs to be "managed" with some new "solution." Customer relationships are the sum and the result of all your interactions with the people that keep you in business. Business relationships are usually built and nurtured over many years by dedicated owners and employees. Thinking about them as just another marketing task to be managed is a recipe for disaster.

Adopting creative listening

Every business has periods when sales decline. This is when they are most vulnerable to being sold a quick-fix technical solution. As most experienced business operators know, the reality is that bringing back sales growth is an incremental process requiring some attention to the reasons why sales are not what they used to be.

There are, of course, situations where business declines for reasons completely beyond our control, like a recession or the emergence of a large competitor. But it is those very situations that call for the most creativity and attention to customer relations. Thinking about new services or innovative ways to retain customers starts with the dialogue described above, and that need not be expensive.

Customers have needs that they don't always state very clearly. Listening to them, thinking carefully about what they are saying and how a new service might serve their needs better is what real customer relationship management is all about.

Your customers may complain, for example, about not having enough time. But that perception can arise simply because it takes so much longer to drive anywhere. Addressing that perception by creating and promoting a more customer friendly web site or offering a faster delivery service sends the message that you are trying to help solve their problem.

There's a lot of useful software to keep track of sales and other customer information, but maintaining good customer relationships is still about the common-sense idea of listening to their concerns and creatively coming up with new ways to serve their needs.

42 One-to-one marketing: nice concept, tough to execute

Customers like to receive personalized messages, but not too personal. Most businesses like to offer customized products or services and treat each customer as an individual, but that can get to be expensive and may mean raising prices or reducing profits. Like many things in life, it is a lot easier to describe one-to-one marketing than to actually do it.

The concept of one-to-one marketing is that each customer is to be treated as an individual and that, by using customer databases and marketing messages, sometimes products or services can be personalized to each customer. One-to-one marketing is the final step in refining target marketing for an extremely segmented consumer marketplace.

When your customers come from only a few small consumer segments, the idea of personalized marketing may make sense, because more precisely tailored marketing messages are usually more effective. But the problem with one-to-one marketing is that creating and managing customer databases can get somewhat complicated and expensive. One-to-one marketing using a customer database is not a substitute for traditional advertising, but it can certainly enhance the effectiveness of branding or awareness advertising.

Each business sooner or later has to decide whether it makes sense to allocate part of its marketing budget to building, maintaining and using a customer database for one-to-one marketing, or to just continue to use that money for traditional print and broadcasting messages. There are a couple of questions to consider when making that decision.

What do you know?

Some businesses know a lot about their customers; others know very little. Some retailers and service businesses, for example, obtain customers' names, addresses and what they purchased. But others operate primarily on a cash-transaction basis and do not retain any information about individual customers.

Many businesses that sell basic items like food, clothing, or home furnishings often have information about where their customers live and what customers buy that they could use for one-to-one marketing. A bookstore, for example, could send a postcard or e-mail to past buyers of mystery novels telling them that a new shipment of such novels has arrived.

That can work because of three conditions: the nature of the business is that there are many different types of things for sale (such as books), both inventory changes and customer visits can be frequent, and, in most cases, the general type of product someone buys (such as a novel, a pair of shoes, or a piece of furniture) is not of personal consequence.

But if what is known about customers is sensitive or confidential, such as medical or financial information, or what is offered does not change materially from month to month, then personalized marketing may not be cost effective. In any case, it should go without saying that all information about specific purchases (such as my weekly acquisition of a glazed donut) should be considered confidential and any use of it a violation of the customer's privacy.

What do you want?

If you have a business that is as big as you can handle, or have the desire to handle, then investing in a customer database for marketing in order to make your business grow is probably not a useful concept.

If, on the other hand, you believe that there is some potential for increasing the size of your business and believe that one-to-one marketing can work for you, then begin to create a customer database. But, by all means, proceed slowly. Geographically code a few of your customer addresses to census geography to see what demographic segments are relevant and test a targeted marketing message to a few hundred customers and see what happens.

Unfortunately, some small firms have spent the equivalent of their entire year's marketing budgets on software and database services only to find out that the expense of maintaining such a big system is more than they can afford. If it's appropriate for your business, finding out what works with a small sample of your customers will enable you to expand into one-to-one personalized marketing with little risk and the possibility of much reward.

Use your head, not your wallet

The basic functions of any database-marketing software on the planet can be duplicated on a small scale with a piece of paper, a pencil, and some common sense questions. Before investing your cash and valuable time in buying and learning how to use database management software, write down the names and addresses of ten more or less random customers.

Next to their names write down the answers to these questions: How often did they buy something? How much did each of them spend in the past 12 months? What did they buy and how did they pay for it? Did any of them return something or have a problem with what they received? How much profit did you make from their transactions?

The list of questions will vary depending on your business, but should include some demographic ones as well. Assuming you have answers for most of the chosen ten customers, then write down what you would say to each of them in a marketing message to get them to buy more. (Maybe you don't want to say anything to the unprofitable ones.)

The heart of one-to-one marketing is the quality and effectiveness of the personalized marketing messages, not the data or the software. The success of one-to-one marketing will depend largely on your ability to answer the above questions, customize your marketing messages, and then do the final step. Measure how much your new marketing effort s added to your revenue and profit.

43 Everyone benefits by sustaining a community

Some of the most successful businesses in America do more than sell goods or services; they do a great job of sustaining a community of customers. From a tiny neighborhood store to a giant like General Motors, one path to a long-lasting franchise is to nurture the natural tendency of people to want to be part of a community. Soon this will be easier to do.

Owners of General Motors' Saturn automobiles all across the country can feel that they are part of a community of like-minded car owners just as the residents of a small housing development can bond with their neighbors by meeting occasionally at the corner store.

The interesting thing about this phenomenon is that affinity among customers is almost never created by the business that benefits from it. Customers independently choose to buy from the firm and then connect with each other. Neither the car company nor the corner store chooses its customers. Customers choose them.

But once a community of customers starts forming, a savvy business can do a lot to encourage stronger connections among customers and benefit greatly from the customer loyalty that accrues. From community bulletin boards in a neighborhood store to a newsy periodical that talks about matters of mutual interest, the key to maintaining a sense of community is regular communication.

The concept of affinity marketing has been around for a

long time and has been used by companies that market credit cards, for example, with the name of your college on them. But we may see a greater desire to form communities in the future for the simple reason that people will not be changing their residence as often as they used to.

The longer consumers stay in one place, the more likely they are to get to know their neighbors and in some way become involved in the community. This can work in favor of any business that serves just one community because greater residential stability makes it easier to get to know your customers and become an important part of their community.

We know that there is likely to be less moving around because the Census Bureau annually documents what is easily observed: young people move frequently, but after age 45, most people tend to stay in one place. And the highest population growth rates are now among people aged 45 and older.

From one year to the next, the Census Bureau reports that about one-third of people in their 20s move their residence. But by age 35 it has dropped to about one-fifth and after age 45 less than one in ten people move in a year's time. By the end of this decade, the largest ten-year cohort in the U.S. will be people aged 45 to 54. This is important because, on average, only 9 percent of them will pack up and move in a year.

Since the oldest baby boomers are now in their mid-50s, the highest growth rate will be among people aged 55 to 64, where year-to-year mobility drops to only 7 percent. Not the lowest rate, but close to it. Fewer than one in twenty people aged 65 or older, or only 4.4 percent, will change their residence from one year to the next.

Geographical Mobility 1999 to 2000

By 2010 a majority of U.S. adults will be aged 45 or older, when
mobility is less than 10 percent.

AGE GROUP	NUMBER U.S. RESIDENTS	PERCENT MOVED IN PAST YEAR
20 to 29	36.7 million	33.8%
30 to 34	19.5	22.0
35 to 44	44.8	14.8
45 to 54	36.6	9.3
55 to 64	23.4	7.0
65 & older	32.6	4.4
Average 20 +	193.6	15.4

Source: Census Bureau

So in future years, there will be a big increase among
people who are most likely to stay in one place and either
slower growth or a slight decline among people who move
a lot.

This suggests that helping to build a sense of community
among your customers may be a very worthwhile marketing strategy.

A sense of community only exists when there is communication among members. Things that facilitate its growth
include web forums, an e-mailed newsletter, or an occa-
sional event to bring customers together. For example, book-
stores can form communities of like-minded readers, by in-
viting customers to come and hear a local author read from
his or her most recent book.

The longer people live in one place, the more they want to know about it. So anything you can do to put your business in a local historical context or sponsor an event tied to the community's past is likely to resonate with people who expect to be long-time residents.

Each business must decide how best to nurture a community of customers, but from a demographic point of view, there is no better time to do it than now.

44 The marketing benefits of giving to non-profits

Every community has hundreds of non-profit organizations that depend on contributions to carry out their work. Those organizations frequently approach local businesses for gifts of cash or merchandise, for volunteers, and sometimes for a place to post signs or solicit donations.

Office-based businesses are often asked to participate in raising money for the United Way or to permit the sale of Girl Scout cookies. Grocery stores seem to be the favorite venue for non-profit groups who provide flowers, buttons, brochures, or just thanks in exchange for a donation. And at some point, virtually every gas station has probably been asked to turn over its parking area so kids can wash cars to raise money for school trips.

Business owners and executives are also prevailed upon to sponsor events or serve on boards of local education, arts groups, non-profit health-care facilities, or other community service organizations. There are also national and international charities such as the Red Cross or UNICEF that ask for contributions from businesses. The list is very long.

No business can afford to say yes to every request to donate money, time, or space. How do you choose? Some business owners or managers just go with personal preferences. If their daughter is a Girl Scout, for example, you can bet there will be hundreds of boxes of Thin Mints or Trefoils sold at that business. But after the easy choices, every business, if it wants to stay profitable, must decide where to draw the line.

Another marketing decision

At some point, making or not making a charitable contribution becomes a marketing decision. The question is: will this donation create enough visibility, community good will, or customer involvement to make the contribution a good marketing decision? This is often a difficult decision, and unfortunately, too many non-profit groups don't make it any easier.

You may love opera, but your customers favor bluegrass.

Many times the non-profit pitch is just: "We need a big donation from you." A more helpful approach might be: "Here's the value we can provide your business in terms of good public relations or high visibility in return for your contribution." Just as for-profits do, non-profits need to practice the basic marketing principle of talking benefits and value before discussing price.

Sometimes the benefits are clear. Buying an ad in the program for a local music or theatre company is just a matter of understanding how appropriate the audience is for your business. A bluegrass music festival, for example, will most likely have quite a different audience than an opera series. The question is, which one most closely matches the interests of your customers rather than your interests? You may love opera, but your customers favor bluegrass. You may be an ardent environmentalist, but your customers are not so committed. This is yet another example of why it is so important to understand your cus-

A Generous Society—Donations by Source

These figures do not include any of the substantial non-monetary contributions by U.S. businesses of merchandise, employees' time, or commercial space.

	IN 2000	TREND 1995 TO 2000
Individuals	$152.1 billion	+ 59%
Foundations	$24.5	+131
Corporations	$10.9	+ 49
Other bequests	$16.0	+ 50
Total	$203.5	+ 64

Source: AAFRC Trust for Philanthropy

tomers' preferences and attitudes, and not just assume they are like yours.

Involve employees

Employees are another set of folks whose preferences and attitudes are probably different from yours. It should not be a surprise if workers suggest that a major contribution would be better spent giving them a raise or avoiding layoffs.

In difficult economic times, community service organizations need donations more than ever, but your business may also have less revenue from which to make those donations. This is when it's most important to talk with sales staff, customer service workers, and other employees about which contributions make the most sense from a marketing point of view.

This may be the best time to have a couple of your employees out volunteering in the community and not-so-subtly delivering the message, "We look forward to more of your business." This can be particularly valuable if, while performing some community service, your employees get a chance to talk in an informal setting with present or past customers.

Get promotional benefits

Assuming that you have determined that the charities or other non-profits that you support are of interest to your customers, be sure to include some mention of your support in your sales literature, advertisements, and other promotional materials.

It doesn't have to be much. Just a simple statement like: "We support …" or show the logos of the organizations you're involved with under the words "Contributor to…". This will give needed publicity to the non-profits as well as showing your commitment to those that both you and your customers think are worthy causes.

Needless to say, the promotion of contributions to religious, political, or controversial-issue organizations—donations that are clearly personal—can have negative consequences on a small business. Anything that diverts your customers' attention away from the effective marketing message of customer service along with community service is pretty obviously not a good idea.

45 Customer testimonials can be persuasive

Word of mouth can be a powerful selling tool. But controlling it and measuring its effect is not so easy. One way to get the benefits of positive word of mouth is to obtain customer testimonials and use them in your advertising.

There are several advantages to getting customer testimonials. First, it means you have to engage at least a few of your regular customers in conversation. You never know what insights that dialogue will turn up, because your customers' view of your business is probably quite different from yours.

Second, regular customers should be able to tell you the one or two attributes of your service or products that they find most valuable and that keep them coming back. If you focus on those key customer-defined attributes in future marketing efforts, you will almost certainly get positive results. Third, after using testimonials in advertisements for a reasonable period of time, you can measure their effectiveness on awareness and sales.

The most obvious benefit of a customer testimonial, however, is that someone other than yourself is saying nice things about your business. All of this presumes that the testimonial is freely given. Paid endorsements, usually by celebrities of some sort, are expensive, are undoubtedly recognized as such, and may not have the same impact for a small business as a regular customer's comments.

Find a representative customer

Some of the most effective testimonials are given by people to whom your other customers can relate or would aspire to be. This is the tricky part. If your customers are people who love to cook, for example, getting a testimonial from the chef at the most expensive restaurant in town may not get the desired result. That's because it might give the impression that what you are selling is only for top chefs and not for ordinary cooks.

On the other hand, sincere comments from a person with some culinary training or demonstrated skills in a kitchen might be right on, particularly if the person looks like someone your target audience would like to be. That is one of the many reasons behind the success of Martha Stewart—she is someone her target market aspires to be.

One thing to avoid is straying too far from the demographics of your target market. If your target market is aged 45 to 64, your testimonials could be from a person somewhat younger or older than that, but should not be from people who look or talk like teenagers.

Take time to tell a story

The best testimonials draw the reader in by telling them a story. The punch line, of course, is why the person being written about is such a loyal customer. But the story is what will get people involved in reading your advertisement and become interested in what you offer.

Most long-lived and successful advertisements have always told a story, because that's what people remember. A good testimonial should establish who the person is, what interesting things they do, how they became customers of your business, and what it is that keeps them coming back.

Customer testimonials must, by definition, be a soft sell. This is because customers are not going to be comfortable selling for your business. They won't mind telling their story and including you in it. But they will probably balk at saying anything that sounds like a sales pitch. That's your job, not theirs.

Testimonials must be credible and harmonious

Like all advertising, customer testimonials must be credible. If some customer talks about your great customer service, but you know from all the complaints that it's pretty poor, don't waste your money putting that testimonial in an ad. Nobody will believe it.

Because customer testimonials only work when they ring true, they should only come after you've made sure that if someone responds to the ad they won't be disappointed. Few marketing mistakes are worse than increasing a potential customer's expectations and then not meeting those expectations.

So any customer comments that you plan to use should be in harmony with your other marketing efforts. For example, if one of your main selling points is promptness of service and speedy delivery, then comments on that, and not something like low price, is what you should be looking for in seeking testimonials.

After a customer's story and testimonial (ideally with photo) has been crafted into an advertisement and placed, it can have a long afterlife in promotional literature or posters hung in your place of business. Keep in mind that existing customers are often looking for validation that they made the right choice and they need to be regularly, but softly, resold.

46 Interactive marketing still works—for some

The dot-com mania may be over, but you can still make money with a good web site. This is because the fundamentals of communicating with your customers have not changed, despite new media hype to the contrary. Talking to potential customers in a straightforward manner in a media they prefer still works, regardless of the technology.

If your customers read newspapers or magazines, it makes sense to advertise there. So if your customers use the web to search for stuff, it makes sense to be there as well. The difficulty is that interactive media is so new that what works and when it works is not as well known as with more conventional media.

The central purpose of a web site is to provide an efficient way to converse with your customers, to show in very great detail what you can do for them and to sell your products or services. It may be efficient, but a useful web site is not free. It requires time and attention to make this interactive media work for you. So here are three tips for effective interactive marketing.

Interactive marketing requires support

Just because you create a web site does not mean anyone will ever visit it or that you will get any benefit from it. People have to be told that your site is there, be given a reason to log on, and once there, be able to derive some benefit for their effort.

Collateral marketing in conventional media is essential. Every brochure or business card, every yellow-pages listing, every advertisement and every press release must have your web address and, if possible, a word or two promoting the site. For example: "See our web site for more details and special offers!"

Don't spend a lot of money to link from other web sites, unless you really believe new business will result.

Linking to other sites can be useful and being catalogued by major search engines is important, but not sufficient. Don't spend a lot of money to link from other web sites, unless you really believe new business will result. Your marketing money will probably be better spent using conventional media to promote the benefits of visiting your web site.

Site design and content is critical

Interactive media means it has to be just that. If you have a static and rarely updated web site that only shows basic information such as what you sell, when you are open and directions to your place of business, then don't expect much from it. On the other hand, if it contains up-to-date product information or other useful data as well as e-mail addresses of key employees for detailed inquiries, then it might live up to your expectations.

But regardless of what you put on your site, perhaps the worst thing you can do is overdesign it. The average visitor to a web site will spend about three seconds trying to figure out what it says before clicking away to something more understandable. Clever little dancing icons or flashing graphics will cost you a lot and just obscure your message. The simplest design is the best design. Useful and up-to-date content is what's important.

A reasonably sized web site (without any transactional capability) for a small business should not cost more than $1,000 to $2,000 to create and less than $50 a month to maintain on a server. The big expense for a promotional web site is not in its construction or maintenance, but in the time it takes to create the compelling content that keeps people coming back to your site and subsequently becoming good customers.

Ask why you need a site

This may sound like new-media heresy, but not every business needs a web site. Before spending a dime on your site,

---

Internet-Usage Demographics

About half of all adults used the internet in the past month, but more than three-quarters of college graduates and professional workers have done so.

CONSUMER GROUP	PERCENT USING INTERNET IN PAST 30 DAYS
College graduates	78%
Professional workers	88
Income $75,000+	81
All adults	52

Source: Mediamark

think about what kind of business and how much revenue you expect to get from it. Presumably you would do that for any marketing expenditure. But somehow, with a web site, the feeling is that you just have to have one, if only because it seems like everyone else does.

Some businesses, by their very nature, will get a bigger payoff from a good web site. Firms that provide services such as financial, legal, or business services, for example, can get a big marketing payoff from their web site because what they sell is complicated, intangible and often changes frequently.

But at the other end of the payoff spectrum is your local gas station. What they sell is nearly always the same and you can find out the only thing that changes, the price per gallon, just by driving by. It's hard to imagine any benefit to them having a web site.

Between those two extremes is probably your business. So here are three questions to ask before embarking on an interactive media adventure:

1. Is there information about what you sell (i.e., product features, service components, technical specifications, etc.) that a potential customer would benefit from knowing?

2. Would customer confidence be improved if they could read something about your firm's history and key personnel?

3. Would it be a benefit to all concerned if customers could send in queries by e-mail rather than phone or mail?

If the answer to all those questions is a resounding yes, a web site will be a great investment for you. But if it's no to all three, then spend your marketing budget elsewhere.

47 Interactive marketing is here to stay

Many internet commerce firms are no longer with us, but interactive marketing is here to stay. For those who have access to it, the internet has settled down to its basic function as an interactive communications media and an information utility. From a marketing point of view, using the internet is by no means the only way to talk to customers, but for many small businesses, it may be an effective supplement to other marketing and it cannot be ignored.

The use of web sites and e-mail has become an essential component for most business-to-business transactions, but despite the mountains of hype, it's not a great shopping channel. According to a recent survey by the Pew Internet & American Life Project, only about 45 percent of all U.S. adults even have internet access and less than half of those with access have used it to purchase goods. However, both access and use is higher among college graduates and young people.

What the Pew Project discovered was that over 90 percent of all those with internet access use e-mail, and about three-quarters of users sought information about a product or service. So from a marketing perspective, deciding to create a web site is about on par with deciding to put a sign outside your premises to tell those passing by that you are there and direct them to the front door. Not everyone will see it, but you better have it for those who do come by.

Using e-mail for marketing purposes, on the other hand, is a more complex decision. While nearly everyone who is online uses e-mail, it, like the phone, is most often used for personal communication, and messages from businesses are welcome only in certain circumstances.

For a local business, my view is that both unsolicited e-mail and telephone marketing is to be avoided. However, once your brand name is established, target marketing using e-mail can be an effective companion to more traditional media advertising. It can be an efficient way to reach customers, but there are a few things to keep in mind.

First, for most businesses, e-mail can only be a supplement to traditional ways of communicating with customers. Broadly based advertising is still important because it maintains the awareness of your firm as well as reinforces your brand identity, which is so critical to success in targeted marketing. E-mail or any other form of direct marketing is always more effective when the recipient knows who you are and what you provide.

Second, people have been getting direct mail at home or at their offices for decades. If it's not of interest, they just toss it. The worst thing that occurs is a wasted marketing dollar. But e-mail and telephone calls are different, particularly to someone's home. Unsolicited e-mails or phone calls can often make the recipients so angry that they develop a negative attitude and consciously avoid doing business with you. But there is nothing wrong—in fact there are many things right—with sending an e-mail to someone who wants to receive it from you. People put themselves on e-mail lists every day. But as we all know, it is the customer's right to change her mind, so every e-mail should end with a simple way for recipients to remove themselves from your list.

Third, the most important aspect of any e-mail marketing effort is the content of the message. If your messages are nothing but undifferentiated or repetitive sales pitches, they will be worse than ineffective. They will annoy those people who could become your most profitable customers.

Suppose, for example, that you operate a fine-dining restaurant. It would not be a difficult thing to ask customers two questions either on your web site or when they pay their bill: Was everything to your satisfaction? and, Would you like to be put on our e-mail list to occasionally receive notes from our chef?

All customers should be reassured that you will not ever sell or trade their e-mail address and that you will not send them more than a few e-mails per month. Privacy is an im-

---

Online Activity by Internet Users

More than half of internet users are interested in health-related information.

INTERNET ACTIVITY	PERCENT REPORTING
Send and receive e-mail	92%
Sought information about:	
a hobby	75
a product or service	73
Sought health information	55
Bought a product online	47

Source: Pew Internet & American Life Project Survey

portant part of the trust between any business and its customers. Customers who do sign up, however, can be asked a couple of questions about their preferences.

As in the case of the restaurant mentioned earlier, the content of the messages can vary depending on the customer's stated food preferences. For example, vegetarians won't get messages about meat dishes. However, the entire e-mail list might be interested in new wines, what fresh fish will be available during the following week, what tasty things the pastry chef is preparing, and what talented jazz musician will be playing on Tuesday nights.

Each e-mail message might also contain a calendar showing available dates and a simple reply mechanism with which they can make reservations for an evening in the future. Customers, of course, need to receive a confirmation and a reminder e-mail on the day of their reservation. And there is every reason to send an e-mail after dinner thanking them for coming in and offering a complimentary glass of wine or free dessert on their next visit.

The bottom line is that e-mail marketing can cement the relationship that a fine restaurant has with its best customers, and it can do the same for many other businesses. E-mail marketing works best in conjunction with traditional advertising. A well-designed web site is a must for any small business where the nature of what is provided changes fairly frequently and when having a good long-term relationship with frequent customers is extremely important.

48 Balance your marketing for best results

Balance is as important in business as it is in life. Eating from only one food group is not good for your long-term health and using only one method of communicating with customers is not good for the long-term health of your business.

Before the dot-com bubble burst, it was suggested that the only way to converse with customers was by e-mail. Well, sometimes e-mail marketing works extremely well. But a steady diet of e-mail can have the unintended consequence of eventually shrinking your customer base to only that handful of people who are able to get e-mail, want to get e-mails from you, and then will respond to those e-mails.

The intense fragmentation in today's consumer markets complicates the creation of a balanced marketing program. Because of fragmentation, targeting only those people or market segments most likely to buy is usually a more efficient way to generate sales. But highly targeted marketing has the effect of narrowing your focus to a smaller and smaller group of potential customers.

Too narrow a focus can create a marketing myopia that obscures bigger opportunities. But too wide a focus can create a marketing mush that is simply not efficient. Achieving an optimal balance between highly targeted marketing and more broadly based marketing is not a simple matter, but the benefits are many.

Broad-based marketing is important because it maintains the awareness of your firm as well as reinforcing your brand identity, brand value, and the brand promise that is so critical to success in targeted marketing. If you doubt that, try changing the name of your established business or product and see what happens.

Test before tinkering

About ten years after starting a magazine, its publisher and other managers decided that the magazine's name was too long and not "hip" enough. But before changing it, they prepared a test using two quite large direct-mail solicitations for subscriptions that were identical in every respect except that one used the old name, *American Demographics,* and the other used the new name.

The response rates from the solicitation using the old name were what was expected and what had been achieved in the past. The response rate when the new name was used? There was none. It failed completely because no one was willing to even send a card in for a free copy of a magazine they had never heard of. Needless to say, the name was not changed, but another learning experience was recorded.

What was learned was that part of achieving a balance between traditional advertising and targeted "one-to-one" messages means knowing which one to use first. Not only does advertising create the brand awareness essential to successful target marketing, but it can also create a larger base of customers who can be sent targeted messages in the future.

Every list of customers, e-mail or otherwise, gets smaller over time, and every marketing database needs to be re-

Information Junkies—People with a Graduate or Professional Degree

People who read all that's required to get a graduate degree are almost certainly information junkies. In many states, they are more than one in ten adults.

STATE	PERCENT AGE 25+ WITH GRADUATE DEGREE	CHANGE 1990–2000
California	10%	+ 35%
Massachusetts	14	+ 42
New Hampshire	10	+ 47
New York	12	+ 23
U.S. average	9	+ 39

Source: Census Bureau Supplementary Survey

freshed with new names and new information. People move away, change jobs, or just no longer need or want what you provide. A balanced marketing program devotes some resources to re-selling or up-selling existing customers using one-to-one marketing. However, balanced marketing also means periodically spending money on advertising to add new names to your customer list and build awareness of your brand.

Each type of marketing has benefits and problems. One danger of relying too much on target marketing is list fatigue. Customers who get too many messages from you may tune out your messages. Part of the difficulty of effective marketing is that the determination of how many messages are too many varies greatly from person to person.

What becomes clear in both broad-based and targeted advertising is that the message content is of paramount importance. If, for example, you get a targeted message that is just a naked sales pitch, it may have a very short life between you and the delete key or the trash can. But if both the advertising copy and the subsequent targeted messages have some tips or bits of useful information, then your response to both will probably rise.

Information-rich marketing works better in print media and on the internet because people who read a lot are often information junkies. But it doesn't work as well on television because most viewers expect to be entertained rather than informed.

49

Don't forget to thank your customers and they won't forget you

Write a check for $100 to a local charity or other non-profit organization, and there is a virtual certainty that you will get a nice thank you note and possibly a newsletter or pamphlet to keep you informed about that organization's activities. In addition, within six months to a year, you will almost certainly get a request for another donation.

But think about how many times over the past year you have spent over $100 using a check or credit card on a product or service and never heard from that business again. For most consumers, $100 is a significant outlay, but it's not hard to spend that much for clothes, car repairs, household goods, dinner at a fine restaurant, or dozens of other goods and services.

It is also not hard for each of those businesses to make a list of their first-time customers' and repeat buyers' addresses and send a thank-you note along with a brochure, catalog, or some special-offer promotion. Few businesses do it, so the ones that do gain a competitive advantage, particularly when the number of customers is not what it used to be.

The competitive advantage accrues because of something nearly all business people know. It costs a lot less to get an existing customer to spend more money than to get a new customer to spend anything. Non-profits know as well that it's easier to get past donors to give more than it is to get a gift from someone who has never given before.

The cost of marketing is a substantial expense for any business, so reducing marketing expenses without any consequent reduction in sales is a worthy goal. How can that be done? It can be done by putting yourself in your customer's place and thinking about how much you appreciated a follow-up call or letter after spending a lot of money on something.

It costs a lot less to get an existing customer to spend more money than to get a new customer to spend anything.

Since much of our economy is now made up of highly competitive service businesses, service providers will be more likely to succeed if they make sure a customer is happy when a service is delivered. It doesn't take much. From your veterinarian, for example, it could be a note thanking you for bringing in little Fluffy and asking if she's feeling better now.

But whether it's a postcard, a phone call, an e-mail or a thank you note, any follow-up communication to customers always sends a message that you appreciated their business and hope to see them again soon. It can also help to cement your business relationship with those customers and ensure that they think of you first when the need arises.

Sometimes the ability to communicate by e-mail can solve a regular customer's problem, avoid an expensive service call, and build a more trusting relationship.

The National Public Radio program *Car Talk* is immensely successful partly because it allows people to ask questions (and sometimes even get answers) about their cars that they

Consumer Spending Growth

YEAR	PERCENT CHANGE FROM PREVIOUS YEAR
2000	+ 4.85% (actual)
2001	+ 2.87
2002	+ 0.22
2003	+ 3.14
2004	+ 4.11
2005	+ 2.84

Source: Economy.com, alternative 2 outlook

could have asked at their local auto repair shop, if they had a better business relationship.

Thanking your customers is important at any time, but when consumer confidence and consumer spending are declining, that little gesture can make the difference for many small businesses between an acceptable selling season and one that is not.

Economists predicted that for Christmas 2001 consumers were likely to spend less at stores than they did in 2000, and they were right. When that happens, consumers tend to be more selective and favor those places where they have shopped before and been treated well in the past.

So here is the rule of thumb. When a customer spends over $100 with you (or a higher figure, if that is more appropriate for your business), send out a thank you note within three days. If you're in a personal-service business, include a query similar to the veterinarian example above and a response mechanism, such as a return postcard. Your customers will appreciate your concern.

One way to find out just how well this works is to include a personalized coupon for the customer to use on the next visit. Coupons are often used to bring in new customers, and they can be effective for that purpose. But coupons are seldom used to thank regular customers, where they can help to build and maintain important customer relationships.

When consumer psychology is in a fragile state, the relationships you have with your customers may be as important to them as they are to you. There has probably never been a time when it has been more important to make the small gestures that build relationships, like saying thank you.

Thank you for reading this book.

Selected Sources

There are hundreds of places to obtain consumer data. This is a selected list of a few of those places that provide information about U.S. consumer markets.

DEMOGRAPHICS

American Demographics **magazine** (www.demographics.com) For more than 20 years this publication has been devoted to keeping its readers up to date on U.S. consumer markets and how they are changing. The magazine is published monthly; articles can also be obtained online. *American Demographics* also publishes an annual source book of marketing products and services. For a subscription, visit the web site or call 800-529-7502.

The U.S. Bureau of the Census (www.census.gov) This is the mother lode of demographic data. The American FactFinder section of their web site is a user-friendly way to find 2000 census data about any geographic area and get tables of data from the Bureau's annual survey programs. There must be thousands of reports and tables of data on their site, including historical information and population projections.

Claritas Inc. (www.claritas.com) One of the oldest and largest providers of demographic and other marketing related data, Claritas also provides software and a lifestyle segmentation system called PRIZM. Claritas is part of the family of the VNU companies that provide a wide range of marketing and media information worldwide. Reports for individual geographic areas can be purchased at (www.connect.claritas.com).

Third Wave Research (www.thirdwaveresearch.com) This firm has developed a user-friendly web site in a partnership with Microsoft's small-business portal: bCentral (www.bcentral.com). The site is highly interactive and offers tools to access demographic data, business data, and purchase-behavior data for virtually any geographic area. The bCentral site also offers short articles that discuss how a small business can use the tools.

Woods & Poole Economics, Inc. (www.woodsandpoole.com) Every year, this firm publishes updated demographic projections for all U.S. counties, metro areas, states and regions, in a three-volume book and on a CD-ROM. In addition to age and household income data, Woods & Poole also forecasts retail sales and employment by industry. These data are not yet available from their site, but can be purchased for one or more areas by calling 800-786-1915.

PSYCHOGRAPHICS

SRI/VALS (http://future.sri.com/vals) This research company has developed a consumer segmentation system that describes consumers in terms of self-orientation and resources. Their description of eight different types of consumers is very useful for understanding consumer motivations and for crafting more effective advertising messages. SRI also provides data specifically for buyers of financial services through its Consumer Financial Decisions Group (http://future.sri.com/cfd).

PURCHASE BEHAVIOR

Bureau of Labor Statistics Consumer Expenditure Surveys (www.bls.gov/cex) This federal agency surveys about 7,500 households a year with two types of surveys. One is a quarterly interview to ask about what the household bought, and the other is a weekly diary to get details of frequent but often small purchases like food. Annual data are on their site back to 1984. This purchase-behavior data can also be found on the Third Wave Research /Microsoft site.

MEDIA PREFERENCES

Mediamark Research, Inc. (www.mediamark.com) This firm surveys over 25,000 U.S. adults annually and provides extremely detailed audience data for consumer magazines, television networks and many shows, major online services, and other media. This firm provides more than demographic data for media audiences; it also offers a vast array of purchase behavior data by product category and brand.

ECONOMIC DATA

Economy.com (www.economy.com) This is perhaps the most understandable and user friendly provider of economic data—the only data denser than demographics. Their site provides, besides many data series, a three-page economic snapshot, for more than 300 metropolitan areas and all fifty states, called Précis. These short reports, which combine text, graphics, and tables, are instantly clear and contain a unique mixture of demographic and economic forecasts.

GEOGRAPHIC DATA

Mapping Technologies International (www.mapus.com) MTI is an innovative value-added reseller of ESRI geographic software and data. They provide training or seminars on how to use this software and offer services, for small firms, such as customer address coding. They also build and install quite sophisticated geographic information systems.

MARKETING INFORMATION

The American Marketing Association (www.marketingpower.com) This membership organization offers seminars, conferences, and publications, primarily for marketing executives. They also offer a wide range of marketing tools and services that may be helpful to a small business.

Index

About the Author

Peter Francese is the founder of *American Demographics* magazine and author of the books, *Capturing Customers* and *Marketing Know-How*. His previous column, "People Patterns" appeared most recently in the six Regional editions of *The Wall Street Journal*. Nationally recognized for his contributions to these publications and his currently syndicated column, "The Marketing Advisor," he speaks and writes frequently on consumer trends and customer behavior. Using examples from a wide variety of business categories, he writes clearly and often with a touch of wit, always reminding readers that the tools they need to improve their marketing are well within their reach. Mr. Francese is a graduate of Cornell University.

The author can be reached at peter@francese.com.